Praying in Time

REV. ROGER A. SWENSON

Praying in Time

IGNATIUS PRESS   SAN FRANCISCO

Cover design by Roxanne Mei Lum
Cover art by Christopher J. Pelicano

To

the people of

St. Anthony of Padua Parish

Contents

Foreword

Prayer is our lifeline to God. Only through prayer can we truly listen to the voice of God and respond to him in love. Only through prayer—both public and private—do we gain the courage we need to allow his Word to take root in our lives and the strength we need to live as followers of Jesus Christ.

Although prayer is crucial, many people profess that they have trouble finding the time to pray or keeping their attention focused while at prayer. Father Roger Swenson, in his book *Praying in Time*, addresses the subject of prayer with profound insight, lighthearted humor, and a flair for the practical. He tells of the struggles and joys which others have experienced with regard to prayer. Readers will readily see reflections of their own experiences in these pages. Indeed Father Swenson invites us all to reflect on our lives of prayer with seriousness and hope.

Prayer, of course, is not simply an obligation, it is also a gift. Throughout this volume, Father Swenson stresses how the Lord reaches out to us in love, how he invites us to open our hearts to him and makes it possible to respond to his invitation. One of the Prefaces of Mass, addressing the Heavenly Father, states, "Our desire to thank you is itself your gift." *Praying in Time* gives us a fresh appreciation for prayer as a gift from God.

Scripture teaches us that God's holy will is not far from us; our search for God need not lead us to distant shores and dizzying heights; we find God here and now, in the time and place where we are living. The search for God must necessarily go on in our day-to-day existence. That does not make the search any less an adventure. Father Swenson helps us understand how that great adventure of grace and glory takes place each day in our homes, our schools, our places of work, our Church. May we readily and joyously respond to God's living invitation by opening our hearts to him each day in prayer.

+ James Cardinal Hickey
Archbishop of Washington, D.C.

Introduction

time (tīm) *n.* 1. A nonspatial continuum in which events occur in apparently irreversible succession from the past through the present to the future. 2. An interval separating two points on this continuum.

Prayer slips the net of time. In our best prayers, we are transported beyond schedule and deadline, beyond the circadian demands of nutrition and restoration, to see things as God sees them, to rest in his timeless eye. It is our joy to admit after prayer what might embarrass us in other circumstances: "I lost all track of time." Even our briefest meditations partake of timelessness when they end with a word to God, for he stands outside the continuum of sunrise and sunset; to speak to him we must engage that part of us that is spiritual, that which is timeless.

As practical Christians, we make use of the clock, setting aside a generous portion of an hour each day for prayer, but within that shelter between tick and tock, we need to be free to follow God's lead, or else what we call prayer is simply an exercise in self-motivation. Unless we embrace the questing Spirit and let go of the protective structure of time, we cannot go to God. Of course, he is always listening; when we bind our prayer to the security of time, he is well aware of our self-deception and pities us for our fear of drifting on the eternal sea. Having heard, however, he cannot respond in a manner that satisfies our busy schedule, for we have put our faith in time and not in him.

In real prayer, openness to God's word takes place on

a level of trust removed from the guardianship of calendar and clock. To escape from time in prayer is to make the soul vulnerable, to accept defenselessness in the face of the punishment time has in store for those who disregard its strictures. The world will glare at its watch, letting us know without a bit of subtlety that it has been affronted, discomfited by our flight. Even though our prayer was occasioned by compassion and concern over the pain in the everyday, the day and those who populate it will not tolerate long that deemed impractical and unproductive. Praying people know the cost of prayer, know that when they return from their sojourn outside of time, feet will be tapping in impatience. Time is the world's prison, and you and I have made a break. It will not go easy with us when we are recaptured.

Still, we pray, for we can do no other. Once we have experienced the serenity beyond time's net, we long to know it again, to hear the Amen to our being, to be affirmed in our efforts at right living, to find forgiveness for our failures. This is not to say that all prayer is placid benediction; often the word we must accept will be one of challenge or even chastisement. Yet, even when the Lord tests our vulnerability with an accusation of betrayal, we remain at peace in this conversation; it is the Master who speaks and we value the privilege of hearing a truth that can only heal, a warning that can only strengthen. We rejoice in any word from our Creator and Sustainer for that word is holy and makes us holy. The specific consequences of this most private of revelations will be seen in the working out of our lives after we return to time's domain, but for now, in this place apart, we are certain that Spirit is speaking to spirit, that the invitation will never be withdrawn, that we can come away again.

Two thousand years ago, the One who created time subjected himself to his creation. In Christ, God came to grace our measured existence, and more, to give himself to the rhythm of life and death. No matter how fervently we strive to take wing, no matter how we soar in the dimension of divine intimacy, the Incarnation reminds us that we must return to the place where the Second Person of the Trinity pitched his tent. Until our time is up, our home is here.

Prayer is timeless, but it is also rooted in time; it springs from the troubles and triumphs of our world as it is at this moment. The insights, the solace received in prayer are for the benefit of the life we live today. Thus, all prayer is prayer *in* time. Rather than a plea for a permanent escape from this world, it is an acknowledgment that the unfolding of God's will on earth has a past, a present, and a future. Prayer in time is made up of equal parts of recognition of our ongoing needs and gratitude for the constant outpouring of God's mercy. Here, the faculty of memory becomes operative and essential.

Because pride is such a pervasive force in our lives, we need to be reminded of our weakness and God's power. Our individual histories are stories of how divine providence and human struggle intertwined. Praying in time sharpens our sense of the presence of God where once we had not noticed it and applies the resultant increase of confidence to the present moment. While yearning to pierce the curtain of time, to break into the realm of spirit and communicate with the eternal Father, we know that we live on the same earth on which his Son walked and in which he was buried. The prelude to the timelessness of prayer must be a journey in time back to the day when we experienced the healing touch of the Son, the protection of the Father, the unity of love in the Holy Spirit.

The stories in this book are based on memories of God

reaching into time to draw forth human courage and hope. The reader should not get caught up in a comparison of details. The minutiae of memories are secondary to the central theme of God's abiding and active involvement in our lives. You may have never been in a hurricane, but you have shuddered in fear at the unchecked power of nature. Your husband may have missed the war, but you have known the loneliness of separation. You have had a good friend; you have been crushed by sorrow over sin. Half-forgotten feelings will spring forth as you rest in these reminiscences; with them will come evidence of God's compassion and grace, evidence essential to authentic prayer. See these meditations as a series of gentle reminders that the God whom we seek beyond time works in time, that his presence in our past is proof of his presence at this moment. In fact, his work in the world of now is his invitation to come away with him in the timeless concourse he offers to all who recognize his footprints in the sand.

Find here a path back into your life, a path in the shifting sand. Let the soft breath of memory uncover the proof that God knelt beside you when you lay in the dust, that he carried you when despair paralyzed you, that he ran with you in joyous anticipation of an oasis of peace over the next hill. God and you have covered many miles in your journey through time. In these pages you will recall with wonder a crowded inn, a narrow bridge, an emerald highway. It all happened to you, not in detail, perhaps, but in essence, all of it in your day, in your time. Use these memories to escape for a little while the pressures of the moment. Let them lead you out of time to the eternal Now who waits for your praise.

Praying in time will be most rewarding for those who are wise enough to know that all prayer should be praise, and that nothing is simpler than praising God. Not everyone possesses this wisdom; too many seem to go out of their way to make prayer complicated. Men and women of good will have become convinced that if prayer isn't difficult, it isn't valid. Mistakenly linking healthy prayer to the wellness phenomenon, respected guides have imposed on the spiritual life regimens more suited to diet and exercise. Unfortunately, the aims of improved physical and emotional health—self-affirmation, self-control, self-initiative—are out of place in the development of the self-lessness of prayer. Programs, theories, and strategies for prayer crowd the bookshelves of religious goods stores, confirming the suspicion that spirituality has become a growth industry.

The ascendance of method in prayer intimidates the ordinary Christian. He is confused by its complexity. Overemphasis on technique also blesses the ill-starred marriage of prayer and personality typing. "Let's test her to see how she should pray." Disappointment is guaranteed when a prayer plan fosters the myth of perfectibility, offering an end to aridity, consolations by the numbers, progress from glory to glory. Just one more seminar, the purchase of the Level II tape, another chapter in the journal . . . don't give up now; God is waiting to reveal himself to you this weekend at the workshop.

So many of these strategies have at their core a misconception of what prayer is; they promote the illusion that the object devoutly to be wished is a good feeling, a balance or harmony between the supplicant and God. While there is nothing wrong with praying for serenity, it or any other end of prayer is God's gift. To rely on a method of prayer as a means of winning God over to one's point of view is to flirt with the twin evils of presumption and superstition.

Real prayer promises nothing more or less than a listening God. It is not complex, has nothing to do with physical health or psychological integration, does not assure progress or reward. Whether petition, adoration, or thanksgiving, real prayer can be condensed into seven words: "You are God and I am not." This is the alpha and omega of praise, the import of this book. Here the reader, prompted by a Scripture passage and the recollection of a universal human experience, meditates on God's presence in an incident in the past in order to praise God now. That praise may take flesh as a plea, a hymn of gratitude, a lament over brokenness, but the conclusion is always the same: "You are God and I am not." The articulation of the radical difference between Creator and creature slips the net of time and carries the praying person to communion with Divinity.

You are ready to embark on a journey in time that can lead you, God willing, to escape time. The road begins in the age of our spiritual ancestors, winds through the hills and valleys of your own experience, and ends in an out-of-the-way place, a place of quiet contemplation where God is waiting to lift you up. It would be wise to choose that quiet place first because you will want to be there when God responds. He will speak of many things, but you probably won't understand his words until you leave your haven and step back into time. Then, amid deadlines and schedules, God's answer will be revealed as you make his will your own. You will come to see that he was always there in the funny and sad situations of your personal history; you will be confirmed in your faith that He is here now, still waiting to hear you praying in time.

R. A. S.

Quality Time

There is an appointed time for everything,
    and a time for every affair under the heavens.
A time to be born, and a time to die;
    a time to plant, and a time to uproot the plant.
A time to kill, and a time to heal;
    a time to tear down, and a time to build.
A time to weep, and a time to laugh;
    a time to mourn, and a time to dance.

(Ecclesiastes 3:1–4)

A sentinel in the hallway, ramrod straight in its vigilance, discreetly taking the measure of life flowing past, the clock had long since become a member of the family. Older than the children and some of the grown-ups too, it provided the soothing sound that many a night relaxed tiny eyelids tight with fever. In a discordant world of randomly slammed doors and impatient telephones, the steady ticking reassured little ones that life was meant not for chaos but for serenity, taught them the calm consideration of each minute in itself, an unpretentious blessing bestowed by a kindly grandfather upon a racing heart unused to innovation. And always, the promise of more to come, a pledge of endless morning.

To the older child, the marking of the minutes mattered not at all. Much more important were the quarter hour chimes, starting pistols for the race to school or the dinner table, death knells at the front door when a good time had lasted too long and the crescent moon became sharp as the blade of a guillotine. Then the clock was for pointing to by an enraged father in robe and slippers offering the victim a short course in time-telling. How many still carry with them the face of an old clock reddened in anger and crisscrossed by veins purple with exasperation?

In its simple loyalty, parents saw the clock as a valued friend, a sturdy symbol of the practical, no-nonsense characters they assumed for themselves. There was a certain nobility of purpose, a measured conscientiousness that matched an adult's sense of duty. After so many years, perhaps bridging generations, the mechanism hidden behind that honest face still told out its responsibility; the pendulum completed another million swings and began the next, the counterweights rose and fell with tidal regularity. And more: here was the best of friends, one that needed another's hand each day to insert the key and revive its drooping spirit, for all of this utility was dependent on a higher mind, a free and flexible mentor capable of providing twelve good turns of the key and not one more. A true friend needing just a bit of consideration at eight in the evening, then willing to serve another day without complaint. The best of friends, indeed.

For some there dawned the day when the unvarying pace of the ticking from the hall became a threat. The ache in stiffening limbs, the murmur of a tired heart lost their match with the stubborn precision of self-shining gears and the crisp report of another hour surrendered. For those who would "not go gently into that dark night", the hour hand was a glinting knife slicing at the fragile lashings that held life together. The mechanism no longer moved sedately but seemed to whir, to buzz with impatience, a chatterbox too eager to broadcast the bad news. No more the steady comrade, the discreet sentinel turned into the town crier, letting on to family and friends the secret that a Niagara of color rinses had not washed away. Once-welcome chimes, warm with the promise of morning, now signaled the approach of midnight.

The old clocks—the stately grandfather clock, the squat ship's clock arched like a wave on the sea, the baby grand, square-cut and columned upon the mantel—had character and projected a personality, an individuality bent on important business. They also gave themselves to partnership. As they ticked and chimed, they wound down, required daily encouragement. "Yes," you said as you approached with the key, "you are a member of this family. You are one with Baby and Junior and Gramps and me." And the clock responded by telling the truth one more day, the gospel of hope and righteousness, of death and resurrection.

Today, a clock is an uncertain visitor in the home. A cold heart of quartz wrapped in plastic competes with mass-produced siblings in every room of the house. Revealing just this minute, beeping the hour, unsure of what the others are saying, always wary of the electrical storm, our throwaway clocks blink nervously in fear of the next whim of design, the next revaluation of color and shape that will relegate them to basement or workshop or the Goodwill truck.

The old clocks, the real clocks were above time, hastening departures, slowing expectation to match the rhythm of the turning earth. Their computerized counterparts are toothless poodles at the mercy of the times; they will not snap at the latecomer for fear of offending biorhythms, souring the season, inviting replacement by a more tolerant transistor molded in mellow pastels. Rather than announce an hour that will never come again, they insinuate a myth of eternal return, easy in their judgment, profoundly

19

anti-Puritan. Some are unembarrassed deceivers, newborn grandfathers, eight feet tall, towers of bezeled glass and burnished filigree, set in two hundred pounds of the rarest cherrywood concealing a three inch powercube with a microchip heart. And all of them, great and small, making of time a plaything, a distraction, one more diversion in a world rushing pell-mell through the day.

"There is a time for everything, . . . a time for every affair under the heavens." The clocks we knew neither deceived us nor lulled us into forgetfulness. Things changed every day, appointments were kept, examinations were missed, hearts were broken, people were born and died every day under the watchful eye of the sentinels in the hall. They quietly chided us for believing we could set the agenda and loudly chastised us the minute we were late. Our revenge was compression molding and designer colors, yet the measured ticking of the Father's clock still sounds in our hearts, still measures the minutes from here to eternity.

To pray *with* the clock seems a contradiction. The best prayer has a quality of timelessness leading to that welcome surprise at the end of a meditation: "Only ten past? I felt I was with the Lord all evening", or the reverse, "It seemed to be but a flash of presence and here an hour has gone by." Indeed, authentic prayer takes one out of time, but preparation for any prayer must take the clock into partnership. Over the long run, fruitful prayer must be premeditated. Praying with the clock means setting a time, preferably the same time every day, to lower yourself into the depths of God's waiting heart. So many of us make the first step a misstep by resolving to pray each day at the first opportune moment. It won't work. Very soon, each day becomes a series of missed opportunities, recognized only at the end when we are too tired to lift a hand in the Sign of the Cross. The contending pressures of job, housework, homework, family needs, and spousal affection squeeze every minute out of the day. The result is that some who give up on prayer are really surrendering to everybody else's schedule, allowing the clock to become a temporal tyrant when it should be a prayer partner.

Instead of complaining that there are only twenty-four hours a day, the person who is serious about prayer rejoices in those 1440 minutes and makes a modest accommodation: fourteen hundred for family, job, sleep, and leisure, forty for prayer. This could mean twenty minutes in the morning before anyone else is up, twenty minutes at night when all is quiet. The proportion depends on one's internal clock. If you break out in cavernous yawns at 8:00 p.m., better to do the lion's share of your praying when the sun is on the eastern horizon, or stop for fifteen minutes after lunch in the church near your office. The important thing is to see the clock as giving permission at the same time every day to put all else aside. You needn't go as far as the busy lady who wears a wristwatch and a lapel watch with a personal alarm. The latter is set permanently for 1:00 p.m. when she leaves the floor of her greeting card store and repairs to a quiet room furnished with packing crates, file cabinets, worn display cases, one Bible, and one chair. A fanatic? No, just a pilgrim who has seen herself come apart at the seams without the felt presence of the Spirit and needs to refresh her sense of direction on a daily basis. Whatever your circumstances, remember the watchwords of prayer: regularity and reasonableness. Let the Father's clock keep you on his schedule each day, every day. Cling to the prayerful proportion, forty over fourteen hundred.

There is a time for everything under heaven, but some

times are more important than others. Christians who proclaim God as the center of their lives know that they must routinely speak with him, learn from him, and rest in him or their agenda will have no spirit. Like all trendy phrases, "quality time" covers a multitude of whims, but the praying person is convinced that true quality lies in a gift measured in minutes yet suffused with the eternal. It is a blessing bestowed by the One who is above time. It is that respite snatched from the demands of a busy schedule on which all schedules, all times depend.

❖

A moment, Lord, just come my way
across the stormy ocean of this day
to shelter from the surging haste,
and with your calming words allay
suspicions whispering of time awaste.

This island, make it your domain
amid the crashing waves of loss and gain;
bestow on me an hour of peace,
serenity in place of vain
conceits, from sterile deadlines sweet release.

Lest respite build too soft a nest
and I would make of you my prisoned guest
enisled by silence in the lee,
remind me, Master, that the test
of prayer comes only in the restless sea.
                    Amen.

The More Things Change

Of old you established the earth,
  and the heavens are the work of your hands.
They shall perish, but you remain
  though all of them grow old like a garment.
Like clothing you change them,
  and they are changed,
but you are the same,
    and your years have no end.

(Psalm 102:26–28)

You knew it was silly every time you walked up to a marquee. "Good money after bad", your mother said. Though she was always a bit off the mark when it came to old sayings, the deeper meaning in her complaint didn't escape you. But it was your good money and you would spend it as you saw fit. Besides, wasn't she the one who told you to get out from underfoot? At first, you haunted only the newsreel theaters downtown; then, as your hopes ebbed with the summer heat, you began to pay the big prices at the feature houses: seventy-five cents, sometimes a dollar, the gauntlet of inquiring eyes as you left before the Oscar-winner started. How often you felt like telling the staring usherettes that you paid your own good money and could leave when you darn well pleased.

That long streetcar ride, a dozen newsreels, some of them repeats, and then the ride home to face more stares. Finally, it all came to a head at supper on the last Saturday in September. Pop had kept his peace since V-J day, but he must have been doing a little calculating. "If you want to waste your time at the show every single Saturday afternoon, that's your business, but I certainly don't think Frank wants you to go through all his money before he gets home. You must be spending five dollars each and every Saturday, and for what? What if you do see him, then what?" It was closer to ten dollars, but admitting that would make you look even more foolish. So you sat silently, unable to defend the indefensible with this day's troopships lumbering across your inner vision.

When they dropped the Bomb at the beginning of August, you had expected Frank to come slamming through the screen door the following Tuesday. At the latest, Thursday. After two weeks of constant fidgeting during which the whole family became progressively more uncomfortable, you were taken in hand by Mom who led you into the dark parlor and made you sit up straight on the edge of the leather chair. It was one of those "Now, you look here, young lady" monologues designed to talk some sense into your hard head: Sweet reason dictated patience. Your father hadn't come back until eleven weeks after the Armistice and he was only in England. Frank was on some unpronounceable island right next to Japan. It could take months. And stop running to the post office for the mail. Your father likes to open it first. Get out of the house. These things don't come over the phone. Get back into the Sodality. Mrs. Stranski says they're dying for new blood on the quilt committee. Your father and Lester get nervous with you mooning around the house every weekend. I just hope you're not driving Mrs. Lucchese crazy at the mill.

So it was their idea in the first place, sort of. In the beginning, your new appetite for the movies removed the fly from the ointment. You sat in the dark of the Avalon or the Jewel and patrolled the decks of every ship that San

Francisco newsmen thought would make a good picture story. You scanned each face as it bounced down the gangplank framed against a duffel bag. At home, Pop continued painting the front room and Lester played cards with his smart-alecky friends in the basement after school. Very soon, the calculating started. Your new vocation was much more expensive than sewing with the Sodality. And it wasn't healthy either. Mom said you were looking peaked. Finally, Lester began comparing your reports of the stars and story lines with the movies he'd seen. One day, Mrs. Gandolfo called to announce that the Gold Star Mothers had eaten at the Broad Street Grill the preceding Saturday; in the space of an hour and a half, she and others had seen you visiting three different movie houses and wasn't that a little strange?

It *was* strange. Every time a dyed blonde broke free from the M.P.'s and ran to embrace a soldier, you felt Frank's arms around you; all the fading sensations of your month together were rekindled. After three years, they still came back strong, so strong that sometimes you thought you were going to pass out. You were in your room over the garage again—the Honeymoon Suite, Frank called it—pushing away the induction notice with the power of love. You would look away from the screen, away from the face that wasn't Frank's to the face that was. It was all you could do to keep from moaning. Lowell Thomas' confident bark fell to a permissive whisper. It never lasted long. Next up were styles for the fall season followed by shots of another factory converting to peacetime production. Stranger still was how quickly the memories fled when you stepped again into the busy street. Then you felt as if you had never met Frank, that your hurried honeymoon was just a dream or perhaps some fading image of a movie whose name you had forgotten.

The day the letter came from Hawaii, you saw your last newsreel. It wasn't even a Saturday. You found the flimsy little V-note on your bed when you got back from the mill on a Monday in late October. Short and sweet, as they say. He was just boarding ship for San Francisco. He loved you and would probably see you before Thanksgiving. Your mother hugged you and said "Thank goodness"; she really meant it. Pop wasn't home yet and Lester was playing poker in the basement. Mom thought you might want to run over to Clare's and the two of you go downtown to eat. Clare hadn't heard anything about her Dave since May or June.

Clare wanted to see *The Best Years of Our Lives* again, but something held you back, something to do with homecomings. You settled on an Abbott and Costello, the first feature you sat through for months. You came in late and missed the newsreel; at the end, you jumped up, but Clare pulled you back. "Maybe we'll see them both." Another troopship, another gangplank, another thousand bouncing duffel bags. But this time, when the blonde broke free and made contact, you saw not Frank's face but that of Dave who had been your steady during most of your junior year. The next soldier was Harold, then Rick, then Martin. Frank was missing when you closed your eyes too. The room above the garage was all done in chintz just as your old room in the house had been. It was empty. The next morning you saw Mrs. Stranski coming home from Mass and asked her about rejoining the Sodality.

Frank must have spent every waking hour in California writing letters. You got one each day for almost three weeks after he landed. You suspected there was nothing else to do as he waited for demobilization. You read the first two; they were filled with Frank's dreams for a house and Frank's gratitude for being spared and Frank's boyish love for you. He never asked why you didn't come to the Coast as Clare did to meet Dave. You supposed that somewhere in letter nineteen or twenty he wondered why you didn't reply. You opened each of the others but put them in your cedar chest unread.

It was funny that he came home on a Saturday afternoon. You weren't feeling well so Pop went to the depot alone. They got back awfully quick. The screen door slammed and he gathered you in his arms just like in the movies. You closed your eyes and saw that cute Dwayne Miller down at the roller rink; you'd been skating quite a bit during the last few weeks.

❖

To a changeless God, a prayer of puzzlement: How could Simplicity itself create such a changeable people? Sometimes it seems as if our personal history is really a chain of disparate lives lived by the persons we have been. Who was it that occupied my room as a teenager? If I met the person I was when I got married, would I recognize myself? Old photographs might make us start or cringe for the amusement of friends, but inside we wonder what that person was like, that hellion in the crew cut, that angel in the prom dress. The name is the same as mine, but what was behind those dewy eyes?

Because the art of retrospection is so inexact, we tend to be swayed by appearances. If the person I was is defined by how I looked and what I wore, by my state in life or state of health, then I should observe closely others now at that stage. Perhaps I was like them. And, indeed, we may gain a fleeting glimpse of ourselves in the persona of a younger pilgrim. But there is another side of you and me that becomes evident only through the inward glance: that which never changes. A meditation on the continuity of one's identity reveals a certain thread of self that stretches unbroken through all the years. Variations in height, weight, age, residence, and employment may mask individuality's persistence as May turns to September, but there are points of proof throughout life that tell us that we are the same person we started out to be. These are moments of crisis, times of trial through which we struggled, seasons when the earth buckled and it was whispered, "He will never be the same again." We may have believed it for a while, yet when the wounds healed, we were the same . . . wiser or sadder, but the thread of self was not broken.

We should thank God often for the grace to grow through the turning points in our lives. We did take a new direction, began to perceive the world differently because of the crises or opportunities that came our way. God was with us, and we were able to go beyond endurance and survival to responsibility and maturity. We are grateful to God for calling us to new insights and commitments, but we never forget the other side of God, that changelessness that is reflected in our abiding identity. It is that irreducible core of singularity that is the sign of our divine creation and the warrant of our immortality. Growth in the midst of trial, flexibility in the face of challenge, no matter how providential, are still earth-bound triumphs. That which lasts is the spark of the divine, that spirit that speaks to Spirit, that *you* that has existed since your beginning and that will exist forever. There, at the still center of your being, is your constant prayer, a silent communion, the changeless embrace of creature and Creator, your eternal "Abba."

❖

far down
deeper deep beneath
under the laminate of life
spoken to One
spoken to One alone
        to One Alone

a word so silent
sounded only in being
        so still
answered only by Being
        only by being

a lasting word
the last word
the Amen uttering
        I
    I whispering
        Amen.

O Happy Fault

While he was still a long way off, his father caught
sight of him and was filled with compassion. He ran to
his son, embraced him and kissed him. His son said to
him, "Father, I have sinned against heaven and against
you; I no longer deserve to be called your son." But his
father ordered his servants, "Quickly bring the finest
robe and put it on him, put a ring on his finger and
sandals on his feet. Take the fatted calf and slaughter
it. Then let us celebrate with a feast, because this son
of mine was dead, and has come to life again; he was
lost, and has been found" (Luke 15:20–24).

Outside, arches of plaited pine boughs stretched across the
street at every lamp post. Nesting among the fragrant nee-
dles were whorled bulbs thick with light, red and yellow
and orange warming the icy night with a promise soon to
be fulfilled. The few people slouching down the quiet sidewalks were distant kin of the frenzied shoppers who had
made their last-minute purchases this morning. As every
year, the merchants had agreed on noon as closing time to
permit men and women of good will to begin the slower
rhythms leading to the chimes at midnight. There were no
shopping malls promising bargains on the edge of town until nine p.m. There was only one place to go on this chilly
vigil; past the locked stores, past a dozen mechanical Santas

behind frosted panes, past the warmth of childish expectation, to join you hugging a heaving radiator in a line curling twice around a clammy nave.

What kind of church was this anyway? Your annual question silently shouted against the scrape of frozen feet polishing the terrazzo. What kind of a church that heralded the birth of a Savior, the warm morning of hope for all humankind, by commanding your presence in a little box to number and name your hopelessness? What a way to run a railroad, to dwell on derailments when the station was in sight.

Here, it was hard to find that cheery spirit that poured out in such abundance from the windows on your way. Here, a hearty greeting was a nod when downcast eyes met by accident. A cough, a sneeze, the snuffling of runny noses played coda to the chaste lullabies of last night's coatless carolers on your porch. If these good deeds did not go unpunished, what hope is there for the evil-doer?

Not that you didn't know the reason for the ritual. It was an exercise in purification; one had to be made worthy to receive a gift beyond value. But why take it to the bitter end? It seemed quite enough to be marshaled with the other malefactors, more than sufficient to spend two hours moving step by ignominious step toward the glinting guillotine, the fate you so richly deserved. Your presence said it all: "I stand in this sorry assemblage because I am one of you. I have done the same and then some." That should be enough. God already knew, and now they did too. Why did purification require the blade to fall?

This inner protest made it worse, convicted you not only of perversity but of cowardice as well. There was a daring alternative. You had seen it happen, not often, to be sure, but once or twice: a man, a co-worker at the plant, ten steps from the purple curtain, turns and walks out the

31

door. For a moment, all those vacant gazes into the middle distance converge in shock as they follow his abrupt movements with envy and then sweep the line for another rebel. Who will be next? Who will go home to greet his children shriven with their classes the week before, to his wife who came on Saturday, and sit down beside the tinseled tree hiding a still-blackened heart? Anyone could do it, anyone who had the courage to spit in Rome's eye, sit defiantly in his pew during Communion tomorrow under the disapproving squint of the Pastor, and face the wondering stares of his friends at work on the 26th, the same stares that followed him out of church. Hitler could do it. Mussolini probably had done it. But you shuffled forward. Seven to go.

The Babe was innocent, and you were not; that was all there was to it. Up there in the gloom of the altar, where the ladies of the Altar Society had worked and argued this morning, stood an empty crib lined with straw. At midnight it would receive its burden. Like a warm golden bulb among the pine boughs over the street, a light would shine forth to be reflected in the scrubbed faces and souls filling the pews. You had to reflect that light or it would become a revealing ray silhouetting the stains that no amount of private repentance could remove. It had to be this way, for your trespasses cried to high heaven and so must your remorse, to be heard and absolved by heaven's agent. By another man. Three to go. May each of them be in need of a general confession. May they leave the Pastor exhausted.

Unfortunately, the three were the Mesdemoiselles Mulrooney, aged spinster sisters with lace collars. The last was swallowed up by the heavy curtain almost before the first was expelled. Now you were completely unprotected, Sydney Carton kneeling, offering his head: "Bless me, Father, for I have sinned."

Behind the screen, beneath a grizzled fringe of hair, a weary voice imposed the standard penance in plain, unequivocal English, mumbled the absolution in accelerating Latin, then, bending closer to your darkened cubicle, confided in a brogue born in Killarney, "You are a good and humble man. May you have the blessed Christmas you deserve. And don't wait so long next time."

You saved your smile for the sidewalk. Those still holding up the walls would have been affronted by even a hint of cheer in a survivor saying his Hail Marys. You didn't skip, you didn't run as on that Friday afternoon long ago the first time God gave you back your breath. Now it was more fitting to walk briskly and drink in the invigorating air. In the second display window was a crèche with figures dressed in medieval robes. In her dark habit, the Virgin bore a striking resemblance to Sister Bridget who prepared your class for First Confession. Once more she spoke in answer to the brash Donny Clark, the likes of him who dared to question the need to tell his sins to another human being. "It's not so much the telling, Donald. It's what goes before and after. Standing in the line is Purgatory. Hearing the absolution is the first taste of heaven."

❖

A brief inspection of the self-help section at the bookstore reveals a sad truth. So many of these works reach best-seller status because of the great number of desperate readers who don't feel good about themselves. The first commandment of most of these pop psychologies is: "Thou shall not accuse thyself." Of anything. Especially of sin. In this age of analysis, guilt is the hobgoblin of happiness. The solution advances with the inexorable logic of the scientific method. Since feeling guilty is passé, be modern.

Dredge up all those nasty emotions and look them squarely in the eye. In the light of this new day, name them, master them, forget them. Unfortunately, this naming and mastering and forgetting often involves one of two deceptions. Either the act or conclusion that has been eating away at my peace of mind for so long was not my fault: I was the victim of circumstances and thus could not help myself. Or the decision I made concerned a matter that was morally neutral: I thought I did wrong at the time but progress in sociology, anthropology, or medicine has shown it to be as normal as breathing in and breathing out. In either case, I have nothing to reproach myself for. After all, I'm only human.

Responsible Christians know better, know that "Examination of Conscience" is not to be relegated to the lexicon of old-fashioned phrases. Each day, we bend or break God's law; the remorse that follows is neither false nor foolish. We have renounced the covenant of love that binds us to one another and to our God who sent his Son to sign that compact in blood. We have broken faith with our Creator, offended our neighbor, and injured ourselves. That hurts. It is supposed to hurt, to remind us not to do it again and to repair the damage. It is as healthy as the sting you feel when the shower is too hot. Without it you would neither adjust the mixture nor apply the ointment. The nightly remembrance of where you went wrong today is the signal to adjust your ways and seek the balm of reconciliation.

Yes, there is the danger of destructive introspection. That is why the examination should be made in an atmosphere of deepest prayer, preceded by a meditation on God's constant love and followed by heartfelt thanksgiving for his forgiveness. The intimate experience of God's love will assure those of tender conscience that while they may have briefly turned away from him, his gaze was steady, compassionate, understanding. At the same time the praying person will experience the compunction engendered by beholding the betrayal of his greatest lover. After this bittersweet meditation comes the naming of the offenses, not to dredge them up and blow them away, but to state them as facts unworthy of a place in divine logic. Finally, a grateful prayer of confidence in the many scriptural promises of God's mercy, perhaps a walk with the prodigal son down that long road home. Can you feel his heart swell as he sees his father, not fuming behind locked doors, not even waiting dispassionately at the gate, but coming forward to meet him with arms stretched wide?

Here is the healthy heart made whole by the admission of evil done and the acceptance of mercy extended. This process of meditation, examination, and thanksgiving just may be the most intimate of our daily prayers, for here is where we hurt and here is where we are healed. The hopes and dreams on which we spend so much of our prayer time might never be realized. We know that our will may not match God's when it comes to the grand design. We know too our distractions in petitionary prayer and those long periods of aridity in contemplation. But here is one prayer that calls forth our deepest concentration, for our sins have separated us from Love himself, one prayer in which God's will is guaranteed by each of his Son's merciful acts. When it is over, we know both that we truly have prayed and that God truly has answered.

❖

Sin so silent, Lord, against your pleading,
    skeptical of words of mercy,
answers not the constant invitation
    urging reconciliation.

Fearsome is the tiniest admission
    opening a heart to pardon;
thus is squelched the healing conversation,
    left unheard your affirmation.

Give me voice, dear Lord, to name the demons
    deep within my muffled conscience;
fashion from this timid declaration
    our renewed communication.
        Amen.

The Catcher

Jesus said:

"Do not be afraid of those who kill the body but cannot kill the soul; rather, be afraid of the one who can destroy both soul and body in Gehenna. Are not two sparrows sold for a small coin? Yet not one of them falls to the ground without your Father's knowledge. Even all the hairs of your head are counted. So do not be afraid; you are worth more than many sparrows. Everyone who acknowledges me before others I will acknowledge before my heavenly Father. But whoever denies me before others, I will deny before my heavenly Father" (Matthew 10:28–33).

A fragile shoot not yet come to blooming, from this distance a life untasted, yet making deliberate, precise preparations to throw it all away in one nearly hopeless act, one chance to hurl herself at the last moment from the final swing of the glistening bar and seize the outstretched fingers of her partner in this mad flirtation. Even the ringmaster was unsure of the outcome; his voice betrayed anxiety as he hushed the customers and ordered the floormen to strike the net. It fell to the sawdust, a waiting shroud for the waiting crowd to gaze upon in disbelief. A moment to grasp the significance of this folly, then the ringmaster raised his eyes once more to the slim figure so far above and in grave tones made tame any foolishness ever dreamed by anyone present. This slip of a lass would attempt the triple somersault without a net. No one so young had ever done it, no girl had ever lived to feel the final security of her catcher's grasp. And here, in this city, this very night, as a tribute to her mother who had just rejoined the troupe after a long hospitalization, here before six thousand frightened eyes, the truth would be told, the circus owners would be convinced that this part of the program should be retained for the rest of the season. Or . . . or they would be forced by tragedy to the opposite conclusion.

At the barked command of the ringmaster, all illumination was turned off. One by one, the colored spotlights were put out, the bulbs circling the three rings dimmed and died. Now there remained only the glow of the red exit signs, suddenly urgent invitations for the fainthearted to make their way to an atmosphere less ominous. Those who stayed in the darkness made out silhouettes in baggy pants dragging a wheeled Cyclops; clowns glancing upward in apprehension pulled a huge searchlight to the edge of the center ring and backed away. With a snap of summer lightning, mercury vapor arcs filled the giant eye, blasting a white-hot shaft against the opposite canvas. Some remote hand caused the blinding beam to sweep the aeries of the big top then plunge it into the squinting crowd and up again, searching for anyone rash enough to call a pencil-thin pendulum safe haven. She was discovered, found not cringing in terror but bravely wagging a tiny hand to the applause first of the ringmaster, then of the huddled clowns and a crowd pleased to release its tension.

The orchestra, that irreverent congregation of scarlet jackets and polished brass, had been silent for what seemed an hour. Forgotten was the crazy tangle of fanfares and waltzes that had enraged the lions and paced the dancing stallions. Now with the sparrow caught on her perch, a pair of snare drums began to roll, unheard at first beneath the sizzle of the searchlight, slowly building in intensity, becoming the pulse of the people, an insistent staccato in the blood. In the ranks of upthrust faces, few noticed the ringmaster retire, few saw his head shaking in denial.

Gradually, the lazy arc of the trapeze became a semicircle as she put her body into a contest with gravity. The searchlight kept the pace, never letting her strain against darkness. Like a daring child on the playground, she pushed beyond the horizontal until, at the end of each swing, up was down and all those gaping mouths were above her. The drums fell off for an instant as a pinpoint spot from behind the stands revealed the muscled torso of the catcher making his first sortie from the opposite scaffold. Legs locked over the bar, he tested the rigging, measured the distance, swung out to time his arrival at that place in the cosmos, that locus of truth. The drums came up again, increasing their urgency as two forms hovered apart, seeming to seek just an inch more of separation to satisfy trajectory and thrust. The snares gave way to tympani. Her final descent began. The shadowed ringmaster cried above the swelling beat:

"Only one chance, ladies and gentlemen. Without a net, only a single chance!"

As she fell closer to the hungry earth, the catcher made his second rapid swing, adjusting each strap and sinew to achieve a precious punctuality. She came up, he dropped for the last time, she rose well past the point of safe return, and crouched, embracing herself, a babe in the womb yearning for rebirth. She spun. He floated to meet her as she completed her third turn and spread-eagled. Her fingers dug into his wrists. Only he saw the terror in her eyes.

There was just the sputter of the Cyclops shutting down as the ring lights gained strength. It would take a while to remember that hands clasped over mouths were also for clapping, time enough for the bar to begin its slow descent. When it did come, the roar was not diminished by the realization in those who sat close that this gamine would never see forty again. Yet her eyes were still young, sparkling in triumph. The catcher leaped to the ground and, taking a single bow, backed away with his finger to his lips. Alone on the bar, she floated above the waves of praise, knowing he would not tell, smiling, bowing, wondering as she had for so many nights, so many seasons, how long her timing would last, how it would feel when her spotlight had to be quickly doused and the clowns rushed in to play doctor for real.

"It is a fearful thing to fall into the hands of the living God" (Hebrews 10:31). Why can't we pray? "No time", says the busy homemaker. "No patience", says the fidgety grandmother. "No place", says the harried forklift operator. How many of these, how many of us are using the bustle of modern life to disguise the real reason for our lack of deep communion with God? No guts. An inelegant phrase, to be sure, but intelligible to all, even those who have never admitted that the cause of their anemic prayer life is their fear of the One who is the object of prayer.

Surface prayer makes an accommodation with fear. It sets limits, puts up the safety net. Surface prayer is padded with particular petitions and a thousand softened syllables to make sure that God can't squeeze in a word edgewise, to hold at bay the voice that terrified Peter, James, and John on Mount Tabor. Shattering pronouncements from the ground of all being will not be tolerated. Surface prayer keeps one eye on the clock, ostensibly to keep us from missing our next appointment, but practically to warn us that we don't have time for letting go. Surface prayer prevents us from falling into the depths.

It's not easy to keep one's balance on the trapeze of life, but swings of fortune, if unwelcome, are at least familiar. To be avoided is the unknown, the risk that propels us into the naked ether to hang suspended, reaching out for a moment or a decade for the strong hands of the Catcher to pull us to safety. He may be busy with unrest in the Middle East or an earthquake in China, and we shall plummet, spread-eagled to the hungry earth. Better to leave that kind of trust to the monks on Mount Athos.

Prayer in depth must be prayer in trust, must stimulate some sort of attempt at relinquishing our hold on our defenses. Real prayer is like death in that we begin to strip ourselves of attachment to temporal concerns. One day, the bell will toll and each of us will fall into the hands of the living God. Real prayer is a rehearsal for that final abandonment.

There is no easy way to practice prayer as a kind of dying. It requires the discipline of trust, a repeated regimen of detachment that, if successful, leaves us without resources, without cunning, without alternative strategies. It seldom happens all at once; rather, little by little we loosen our grip on the bar, hoping against hope, believing in our unbelief that out there in the darkness are strong hands waiting not to cuff us for our offenses, waiting not to remold us violently into the form of an angel, but waiting to enfold us in love and consolation.

Our trust in the Catcher is not without basis for we have seen those hands before, touching a leper, mixing a sight-restoring poultice, helping a wanton to her feet. We have seen those hands offering the bread of eternal life and pinioned in a sweeping embrace of final forgiveness. It is those hands toward which we stretch in the depth and darkness of the prayer of trust. It is those hands that beckon forth that painful extension of the soul, reaching beyond words and formulas, yes, even beyond Scripture and ritual to the only One who can halt our chaotic tumbling.

It *is* a fearful thing to fall into the hands of the living God, terrible in its risk, terrible in its denial of all we know to be secure. This is prayer at the top of the arc, prayer at the leap, prayer when the drums suddenly cease and all is silence. Here is death before its time, a reckless lunge in the darkness for new light.

❖

a shooting star
a prayer to Thee
a spark through layered mystery
demagnetized set free from fear
but lost in space
its path unclear

a falling star
far off the course
to union with the burning source
of succor consolation love
inviting yet
so high above

a dying star
bereft of fire
a fitful ember on the pyre
of charred petitions for rebirth
for one last proof
of warmth and worth

o David's star
guide save ignite
these poor reflections of your light
which rise and fall and sputter out
ablaze with hope
bedimmed by doubt
    Amen.

The New Order

On the third day there was a wedding in Cana in Galilee, and the mother of Jesus was there. Jesus and his disciples were also invited to the wedding. When the wine ran short, the mother of Jesus said to him, "They have no wine." [And] Jesus said to her, "Woman, how does your concern affect me? My hour has not yet come." His mother said to the servers, "Do whatever he tells you." Now there were six stone water jars there for Jewish ceremonial washings, each holding twenty to thirty gallons. Jesus told them, "Fill the jars with water." So they filled them to the brim. Then he told them, "Draw some out now and take it to the headwaiter." So they took it. And when the headwaiter tasted the water that had become wine, without knowing where it came from (although the servers who had drawn the water knew), the headwaiter called the bridegroom and said to him, "Everyone serves good wine first, and then when people have drunk freely, an inferior one; but you have kept the good wine until now." Jesus did this as the beginning of his signs in Cana in Galilee and so revealed his glory, and his disciples began to believe in him (John 2:1–11).

Finally, you relaxed. Jim had made you so nervous with that early morning call, first waking up Aunt Ivy who was sleeping downstairs on the couch with her head practically on the phone. You heard that funny hollow sound her head made when it hit the table lamp. Sounded like Larry hitting Curly in the Three Stooges. You heard it because you had slept only a half hour or so. Aunt Ivy's hollow head interrupted but briefly the parade of florists, organists, priests, caterers, dressmakers, uncles, cousins, in-laws-to-be, and photographers who tramped through your mind, keeping you awake with an endless stream of questions. You never realized how many decisions it took. So you answered Aunt Ivy's hesitant knock with genuine relief. Ivy MacIntyre never asked any questions. She went where she was told and stayed where she was put, even if that meant sleeping on the telephone.

Aunt Ivy was worried about this call, worried about bad luck. To a spinster, nuptial misfortune was serious business. You had to assure her that the bad luck came only if the bride and groom actually saw each other. The telephone didn't count, unless, you thought to yourself, you were sleeping on it.

As you hurried down the stairs, you convinced yourself that Jim's sunny outlook would be just what the doctor ordered. That's one reason why you were marrying him, wasn't it? He never worried. The wedding plans were a case in point. "You and your mom take care of it. Whatever you think will be O.K. with me. After all, it's your wedding." That's the part that always lit your fuse. It was his, too. But he knew that; he just wanted to get your goat. That morning, though, you were ready for some of his malarky.

It happened that Jim was out of malarky. He was worried for once, but not about music or flowers or hors d'oeuvres. The parade that passed through his head last night didn't have a cast of thousands. There had been only one person on Jim's mind for the past five hours and that had been Jim. He had begun to take seriously some remarks made about the Holy State of Matrimony by cynical friends at Wednesday's bachelor party. Now he was not so sure. The morning of the ceremony, your betrothed of two years was, as he put it, "just wondering". Of course, he stopped using that horrid phrase as soon as you turned on the waterworks. But the tears didn't keep him from telling you that he had had some doubts as long ago as last Christmas. You didn't want to hear any more of that, so you stopped sniffling long enough to tell him that, if he didn't show up at church, you would kill yourself right on the altar. You hung up before you had to name the weapon.

Mom came to the rescue. She knew the gist of the conversation as well as if she had heard it on the upstairs extension. Your dad had done the same thing, she said. All boys get cold feet right before, she said. Jim would get over it, she said.

Sure enough, at church, Jim was back to his old tricks. Everybody could hear him laughing with Father in the sacristy, pretending to accept the invitation to leave by the back door. When he took your hand at the foot of the altar, he winked at bad luck and gave you a kiss. And then for the real one later on, he dipped you so low that everybody laughed. While you were worrying about when to stand and when to sit and *how* to sit in that ungainly gown, Jim was whispering to the best man. Holding your finger stiff and cold, you shook with nervousness while the best man—carrying out Jim's orders, no doubt—pretended he couldn't find the ring. Then it was over, not the Mass, but the important part: "Let no man put asunder." Finally, you relaxed. You admired the floral arrangements, sang the hymns, laughed when Jim did, and smiled at the kisses in the receiving line. Marriage was going to be good for you. It was wonderful so far.

How often you've thought of that double-faced day with

the miracle right in the middle. God came close to you and made you a wife by giving you a new set of priorities. It was a miracle as surely as was the revolutionary method of serving wine that Jesus had introduced at Cana. Imagine, the best coming later! Years after, you would laugh with your friends and readily agree that what you felt was merely relief at landing your man. In your quiet moments, though, you know that isn't true. You've never been able to explain it to Jim, this new system you stepped into, or, rather, were pulled into by the intense presence of God at your wedding in the person of his beloved Son. It must have been like what happened at Cana that day when Jesus did his mother's bidding and turned the customary order of importance upside down.

This new order began when you spoke your vows and accepted your ring. All those worries that had kept you up the night before and plunged you into tears that morning seemed, not exactly silly, but quite secondary. As for the snares hidden in the next few hours—all the things that could go wrong at the reception, on the night's drive, in the hotel room—you knew you could handle them, because it wasn't just you and Jim anymore; it was you and Jim and Jesus.

The power and compassion of Jesus plucked the ceremony at Cana from the edge of disaster by showing people what is important and what is not. The fervor of the celebration, the abundance of food and drink, even the level of mutual commitment of the bride and groom are secondary to the presence of Christ. The rings can be diamond studded, the officiant a bishop, the guests noble, the church a cathedral. If the Son of God has not been invited, recognized, and given a place of honor, the marriage is at risk.

Christ reorders the lives of a man and a woman when he embraces them in the sacrament of matrimony. That was

47

the difference you felt as soon as you had made your pledge of fidelity. That is the difference you have felt in moments of crisis and joy all your married days. It is a sense of priority that has become part of you, a talent for weighing and measuring on God's scale each gift or challenge offered by the world. Think of Mary, wife of Joseph of Nazareth, at the wedding of Cana. See her standing calmly in the frenzy of waiters who know that disaster looms. The sky will surely fall on their heads when the party learns that the nectar of Yahweh, his blessing upon this couple, will be exhausted before the reception ends. What a disgrace for the parents! How embarrassing for the couple to be forced to send their friends home. Mary is not anxious. She asks of her son a favor. Even though his hour has not come, she would have him make known his divine presence. That done and the rest will fall into place. He does his mother's bidding and a new order of things begins to emerge. It is his presence that is the catalyst. All else follows. All else gives him glory.

❖

The end of a quiet few minutes of prayer: Richard must do better in school despite the tyrannical Mr. Powell in math; your mother's arthritis; a safe trip to the coast for Nell and Ed; less gossip at the kaffee klatsch; the repose of the souls of Grandma Netty and the little Hammond girl. What else . . . what else. . . .

When was the last time you thanked God for that amazing mixture of body, spirit, mind, and emotion you've been immersed in for how many years now? The intimate intertwining of two lives for life shouldn't come under the general heading of "Blessings" for which you express sometimes vague and perfunctory appreciation. Instead, this enduring union should be right up there with the new wine at Cana under "Miracles, First Class". Not to put too fine a point on it, you didn't split up yesterday. Of course, that wasn't even in the cards; neither of you has ever been desperate enough to seriously consider separating. But how many couples who let the world order their priorities are filing papers this morning in your city, how many thousands in this land of the free and the home of the no-fault? On more than one occasion, you two have survived arguments that send others to their lawyers. That alone is a miracle worth daily praise.

Consider the miracle of tolerant proximity: you and your partner and the kids in that sardine can of an apartment for so long. About you the headlines never screamed, "Kills Mate and Tots Over Closet Space". Consider the miracle of parental selflessness and all the things you still can't have because you wanted the best for your little flock. Count the marriages that founder on the rock of conspicuous consumption. Consider the miracle of maturing faith in a cynical age; because of your union, and sometimes in spite of it, you are still a praying person. As long as one marriage endures in this era of militant individualism, as long as one couple weighs and measures the world as Jesus did, God's wonders will not cease.

Why, in an age of tenuous commitments, have you been able to keep yours? Because God sent his Son to perform a miracle at your wedding, a work of love that has lasted as long as you've been together, lasted even through storms of sorrow and suspicion when your heart was nearly shattered. Though at times it may have seemed impossible to go on and you had no love left to give, there was never a day without love between you two because Jesus was with you. Even when you couldn't see it or feel it, love was present, love-made-flesh.

In calling married couples to a new order, Christ makes his primary task that of nurturing and perfecting the unity his Father called into being, that shared perception of what is really important. You are part of that communion for you once answered "I do" to the Father's call and still continue each day to respond to his Son's vision of true worth. An Alleluia is certainly proper, a song of gratitude for a marriage made in heaven, proven in tears and forgiveness, still standing the test of time right here in your world.

❖

Accept, O Lord of lasting love,
our praise for blessings soft-bestowed:
for tolerance, long suffering,
for hearts romantic, hopes mature,
for knowing glances, warning looks,
for understanding in the clash
of headwinds on the sea of life,
for deep communion 'neath the waves.
Amen.

And This Is My Friend, Mr. Laurel

A faithful friend is a sturdy shelter;
    he who finds one finds a treasure.
A faithful friend is beyond price,
    no sum can balance his worth.
A faithful friend is a life-saving remedy,
    such as he who fears God finds;
For he who fears God behaves accordingly,
    and his friend will be like himself.

(Sirach 6:14–17)

They were both innocents. Stan's simplicity was easier to see because it was absolute. His was the completely unpremeditated life, free of any thought for the continuing consequences of his actions. Long range, to the artless Mr. Laurel, meant "fifteen minutes to a quarter of an hour". Unbidden and unfamiliar, common sense came to him with the sharp report of a ball bat on his noggin and remained as long as the sting of it. If retention is essential to education, he would not be called a good learner. He could loosen his grip on a balky piano three times before breakfast and be amazed each time it dragged his howling partner down the same flight of steps. Nor was he even the rudest kind of philosopher; the ability to generalize was not one of the arrows in his quiver. The geyser of fire resulting from a drill going through the floor and into a gas pipe could not be duplicated by drilling another hole three inches away. The second whoosh of flame would be like the first, isolated, accidental, never to be repeated. And so he drilled the third. Life for Stanley was an unending kick in the pants, yet despair was not in him, for even as he rubbed his rump, he knew he would never get kicked again.

Oliver Norvell Hardy hid his naïveté behind a conspiratorial wink. He loved to give the camera a brief stare to let the movie audience in on the depth of his partner's ineptitude. Those looks were often partially obscured by falling debris; sometimes only his eyes were visible as Ollie scraped some pseudonymous goo from his face. Unfortunately, the debris, the goo, the ignominy were usually the result of his own plans gone awry; once again he had trusted in the friend who unfailingly made sows' ears of silk purses. At bottom, neither had a monopoly on foresight, but when the dust settled, it was Ollie who should have known better. His memory, though no more enduring than that of a chubby puppy, still operated fitfully. Stan was the man without a memory, and thus, without regret.

This is not to say that Stanley was without feeling, or even thought. He cried suddenly and sincerely over Ollie's cruelties, smiled wide as an English sole when praised, thought so hard on rare occasions that the strain was visible. Yet it was all over very quickly, the whimpering sob, the screechy laugh, the knitted brow suddenly giving way to a blank stare, a face, a mind at rest, no one home, don't bother to knock. He shambled through life with the plug pulled, all circuits shorted out, until, inevitably, there appeared another open socket. Once again, he wetted his finger. . . .

Ollie passed through life with the grace of a three hundred pound ballerina. He was usually quite careful about where he stepped, about his appearance, about his manners. Except toward Stanley, his courtesy was of the gushing kind. In the presence of superiors, shrewish spouses, and officers of the law, he was the soul of tact, mounting a campaign of smiles and patrician gestures until something in the cosmos slipped and a grande dame's dress was ruined. "I seem to have made a slight faux pas", he would murmur, flourishing his tie, even as he saw out of the corner of his eye the next disaster in the chain that would draw him finally into another fine mess.

Ollie's problem was that he could think, not a lot, but enough to make a difference, enough to set him apart from the vacant Mr. Laurel. His reasoning was tactical, not strategic. Well within the range of his talent was the concoction of a story for the Missus about the need for a solitary cruise to Hawaii—"solitary" here being a valid description of an ocean trip with Stanley—as a cover for a forbidden jaunt to a Chicago convention. Foreseeing the need for another story should the liner sink—which, of course, it did—was a bit much for his powers. Had he enjoyed the same mental vacuity as his friend, happiness would have reigned at the Hardy household since there would never have been a scheme in the first place. For his part, Stanley was graced with the protection God gives stray dogs and fools. When the boys returned from Chicago, Ollie, suddenly sensitive to the fire in Mae Busch's eyes, unreeled an even more grandiose lie and was rewarded with a merciless shower of pots and pans. Stan confessed immediately to his Honeybunch, cleansing his reputation for innocence with copious tears. His reward was pots and pans brimming with a welcome-home banquet.

They put up with each other because the screenwriters made them friends in need. Neither held the other under a spell; neither had any money or prestige to attract the other. They were simply washed up on the shore of a life that didn't suffer fools gladly. It is too easy to say they complemented each other. True, Stan's mistakes often allowed Ollie to get a step up, but they were both bottom-rung people. Yes, Stanley often found security in Ollie's public bluster, but the cost in bumps and bruises was high. Each could have gone his separate way and, if not flourished, at least survived. The answer lies in mystery, the mystery of mutual attraction and affection, a communion usually hidden until the end of an adventure. The last scene in *A Chump at Oxford* is revealing. Stanley has regained his senses after spending the final reel thinking he is an English lord and Ollie his manservant. In his strange state, he had insulted Ollie egregiously, telling him he hadn't the manners becoming a lackey and to keep his "chins up". The convergence of that thatched head and the inevitable falling window brings him back to what, in over one hundred films, has passed for normal. His incompetence restored, he allows himself to be hugged. "Stan, you know me!" Ollie burbles, then touches his double chin, remembering the insults, glaring at the camera. Is this a time for tactics, for retribution? No, this is a time for friendship, no matter how unwise. He hugs again the wooden Stanley whose arms still hang at his sides. As always, it takes Mr. Laurel longer to put all the gears in motion, but just to have him back is enough for the grateful Mr. Hardy.

❖

Unless the needs of our friends are immediate and obvious, they tend to be found well down on the list we carry into our daily conversation with the Lord. Whether we are storming heaven or politely seeking a minor blessing, our entreaties revolve around what's best for Number One: first, serenity of soul, a healing of that ache in the heart of yours truly, then a merciful rescue *for* and *from* certain accident-prone family members who live to prove that misery loves company, a petition for sunny skies over my booth at the church fair, peace at the office would be nice and, of course, around the world, don't forget the Pope's special intentions, and finally . . . but time's up, the bus won't wait. I'll remember Vera and Hank and Lottie tonight before bed if I'm not too tired. Besides, they seemed quite all right after church on Sunday.

Take a moment to consider the uniformity of human nature. Because you were hiding that ache in your heart, you seemed all right on Sunday too. Is it beyond imagining that there were similar sorrows behind those smiling faces? Reflect further. God has blessed you with friends for many reasons. Could one of them be to pull you away from too much self-absorption in prayer?

To see how God might invite you to modify your prayer pattern through the silent cry of a friend in need, forget about prayer completely now. Instead, recall a time of darkness when you refused even to think about a God who would allow you to suffer so, for fear you would curse him. Unbearable sadness or worry had undermined your faith in divine goodness. Unable to rise above depression, you gazed bleary-eyed at an unfeeling world. Suddenly, a voice pierced the gloom, not a silent cry but the lament of a friend a hundred times worse off than you that day. Somehow, the habit of Christian concern was energized, a dying ember of selflessness was fanned into flame. Without thinking, you reached out to help. Companionship, consolation, understanding streamed from an inner light that you assumed had gone out when you found no illumination for your shadowed soul. In going to another with compassion, you left behind your troubles to find on returning that they seemed more manageable in this new light.

Apply this pattern to your self-absorbed prayer. By its very nature, prayer will always have its genesis in the praying subject, but its reach need not be restricted to personal

55

salvation. That it must not is made obvious in the High Priestly Prayer found in the seventeenth chapter of John's Gospel. There, immediately before he willingly steps from the murky understanding of his Apostles into his own final darkness, Jesus intercedes for his friends. Plainly, his concern is for others, else he would not be setting out for Gethsemane and beyond. It is the model for your concern on that day when a needier friend stumbled into your gloom. Later, in the Garden, he will ask for strength for himself, but first, like you, he tends to the cares of those without hope; he prays that they might know his Father's protection. His self-sacrificial actions find their voice in prayer for his friends. The circle of prayer for others now completes itself as Jesus finds the courage to endure his trial, for one answer to selfless prayer is a renewed sense of one's own mission. "I consecrate myself for them" (John 17:19).

Since our sense of mission is so often muddled by personal cares, we would be wise to follow the way of the Master, that is, to get away from ourselves in prayer. By means of our concern for our friends, we learn a new way of praying; we learn how to deepen but not lengthen prayer for ourselves, to give more of our prayer time to those who in their silence only seemed to be doing well enough after church last Sunday.

Although we never caught Ollie praying, Stan was no stranger to the art. Now and again he could be found in his nightshirt and long woolen stockings, kneeling at the side of a bed in one or another house of cards. His lips moved but we heard nothing, saw only that brow wrinkled in unaccustomed concentration. Knowing him as we did, envying his absolute confidence in a brighter tomorrow, the blessed certainty that he would never again be kicked in the pants, we had to believe he was praying for someone else, a friend, most likely. And Mr. Laurel had but one.

❖

Come   I
what may   to Thee
O Lord   commend
I pray   this plea
for friends   that those
and say   to me
enough   so dear
away   might see
with self   their hopes
today.   set free.

Amen.

The Still Point

After this, Jesus moved about within Galilee; but he did not wish to travel in Judea, because the Jews were trying to kill him. But the Jewish feast of Tabernacles was near. So his brothers said to him, "Leave here and go to Judea, so that your disciples also may see the works you are doing." Jesus said to them, "My time is not yet here, but the time is always right for you. The world cannot hate you, but it hates me, because I testify to it that its works are evil. You go up to the feast. I am not going up to this feast, because my time has not yet been fulfilled" (John 7:1–3, 6–8).

The hopscotch of starlings seemed more hurried on this gray afternoon. The pattern of their search across the soggy playground was the same as always; the hindmost, sensing no feathered friend to the rear and slim pickings ahead, leaped to a point just in front of the momentary leaders, there to find fresh forage until outdistanced by a new line of suddenly recollected laggards. Today, however, there was little time to pause over a choice of morsels. It was catch-as-catch-can, a flapping ferris wheel driven too fast for decision, hustled along by an urgent wind and curtains of fine rain.

Behind the streaming windows, children torn by the strangeness of things divided their gazes, first peering at the incessant motion of the birds, then turning back to observe the cafeteria and the inert forms of their parents slumped on thin mats against the cement block walls. Think of it: mothers and fathers at school well past five o'clock, driven like starlings from market to gas station to hardware store, driven finally to ground here among short-legged tables and half-sized chairs, bringing sacks of diapers and hampers of sandwiches and mildewed sleeping bags and younger brothers and sisters clutching at the bottle. Outside, the little purple birds still searched for the seed to sustain them through a night coming much too early. Soon, they too would dart to a niche under creaking eaves, some haven just a bit less vulnerable than their own fragile skeletons.

The eye had bumped along the coast all day, probing the dome of high pressure, waiting for its predicted erosion. Midnight, said the forecasters. At nine, in the light from the uncovered windows, the wafting veils of rain turned solid, bent to forty-five degrees and more by the moaning wind. Grandmas shushed their husbands' talk of the storm of '47, youngsters were pulled from the windows to the inside walls, fathers began to stack tables against the shaking panes. At 9:51, the electricity went off, the gauzy purse in each of twenty Coleman lanterns became blue flame, radios were switched to battery operation. Glass was breaking somewhere down the street. Children burrowed into their blankets.

An hour's worth of fiddling with the static-ridden radios produced no intelligible voice; one by one they were abandoned. Now the only rival to the roar outside was a rising murmur growing stronger with each rattling blast, then softening in the lee, whole families matching the fury of nature with the fury of prayer. God was importuned, Holy Mary beseeched to intercede with her Son, a string of patron saints compelled to look upon their quaking charges. Around 1:00 a.m., a dance of lightning revealed the upturned roots of an ancient oak and its gnarled branches embracing a yellow bus. The name of Saint Jude sprung from group to huddled group.

The thrust and parry of wind became wilder, a reckless duel in the dark. The old ones knew what to expect. Many times in this same cafeteria, they had measured the progress of the eye by comparing the severity and duration of the most powerful gusts to the relative calm between them. As dawn approached, there was only an instant's respite between the prolonged onslaughts of the most ferocious winds. The northern wall could not be far away, that towering shroud a mile thick, whirling with savagery unchecked, sustained at well over one hundred miles an hour according to earlier reports. Parents covered the bodies of their young against fifteen minutes of solid, counterclockwise hell.

The first foot-square pane gave up its shivering and spattered the tables layered in front of the windows. Then another and another until whole casements were wrenched away; a wave of glass washed up against other tables set as fortifications around families pressing the opposite wall. Many thought of the high school gym, the official shelter with high, narrow windows and the Red Cross canteen, the haven they had refused, preferring instead to stay in the neighborhood close to their homes. Never in the memory of the ashen-faced patriarchs had this cafeteria lost even one pane of glass. Now, in the glow of the lanterns, they beheld a rising tide of brilliant splinters as the victorious storm hurled lunch trays at their heads. A cry went up, a hundred voices made one in terror, outshouting this hurricane seemingly centered between these four walls. "Jesus, Mary, and Joseph, have mercy!"

They lay with their cheeks hard upon the greasy tiles. So intense was their clamorous prayer that they were unaware of the abrupt silence. Even after some stood up and threw off their dripping blankets, others persisted in the common petition. It was the weak sun glinting on the slivered glass that assured those still sighting along the littered floor. Afraid of a trick, they stepped carefully to the yawning windows, disturbing the sodden starlings under the eaves. As the birds arced into the blue sky to dry their wings, their earthbound cousins stared at the devastation within and without. Many signed themselves, in thanksgiving or in sorrow, as they glimpsed their roofless homes, their overturned cars up and down the street. A few began to collect their belongings, preparing to make the sad journey back to what had been neat lawns and generous porches.

They knew better, of course, knew that once outside in the silken mist of this fresh morning, there would come the clank of an armored vehicle or the roar of a bus picking its way among the fallen trees. There would be a deputy sheriff, barely hiding his disapproval of their choice of shelters, sent to deliver them to the high school. He would say what he didn't have to. "C'mon, people, this is only the eye and you know it. We've got less than an hour before the south wall hits. Any injured?" Even now, in the back of the room under the serving counter, starlings were puffing their feathers, settling themselves.

Sometimes it is prayer enough just to hide in the power of God. To escape for a while a world awhirl with threat and calamity is not an act of cowardice but common sense. Yes, it is good to have a prayer plan for the ordinary days, a series of steps leading to a heightened sense of intimacy with the Lord, but when life becomes a hurricane, the niceties of method fly out the window. With the house payment two months past due, the doctor's prognosis terrifying, the business going down the drain, a battered soul forsakes the latest seven-stage method of contemplation in favor of simple safety.

Peace to the prayer activists. They are quite correct in counseling us to integrate prayer and daily living, to use the slings and arrows of the moment as pointers to a deepening relationship with the Lord of life. Since Christ came to walk among us and minister to the lowly, we should indeed look for him at the checkout counter and in the nursing home. Part of every good prayer is identifying divinity in humanity. But each of us has also experienced the rolling thunder. Blinded by clouds without the hint of a silver lining, we've faced situations in which God's love could not possibly be operative. Evil happens. It has happened to you and me in the presence of a malevolent force greater than we can withstand or understand. At these moments of crisis, our only recourse is to get out of harm's way, to seek a quiet place in the eye of the storm and wait for the Almighty to extend his saving hand.

"You go up to the feast. I am not going up to this feast, because my time has not yet been fulfilled." So Jesus stayed behind, hesitating to enter a Jerusalem swirling with plots. Evil would be done at the Feast of Tabernacles and he would not be ready to withstand it until his hour had come. His habit of constant communion with his Father assures us that he stayed behind to pray. Here is our model for those situations beyond our control. If Jesus used common sense, why shouldn't you and I? Remembering the fragility of our existence, we offer ourselves to our Maker just as we are. True, we have smudged his fingerprints; we are not the pristine souls he set upon the earth so long ago, but we are still his. We still hold a claim on his providence. In the prayer of escape, we do no more than pronounce that claim in the silence of simple need. Our quaking hearts remind God that he is responsible for us; our flight from the naked reality of evil is proof of our powerlessness. We are not going up to this feast of fools because we are afraid.

"Lord, I am afraid." Nothing more need be said. To presume to advise God on a plan of rescue is to withhold the complete submission he desires. Your arrival at this place and time is an admission of your inability to make things better. A chaotic combination of dark events has done something you were incapable of doing for yourself; it made you humble. This is surely not the moment to dictate to the only One who can save you. Your simple prayer has already been answered. You are hiding in his love, letting him hold back the roaring world. You have sought and found the only power capable of resisting the evil that threatened to crush you. It is enough to let the fear seep away. No words of yours can hasten the faith gathering strength in your heart. It may take an hour or a day or many days, but you keep returning to this still point in the storm until your silent prayer ends much as it began. Just one new word is added: "Lord, I am *not* afraid."

"But when his brothers had gone up to the feast, he himself also went up, not openly but [as it were] in secret" (John 7:10). You will go up too, once more encountering the puzzles and problems of daily life. As before, most of your challenges will be ordinary, but now and then a lurking hurricane of evil will strike. You will be more confident now because of what you learned in your secret place under God's gaze, but you will not be foolhardy. Some adversities tower above the highest thunderheads. Shrinking back, you will wisely seek the calm eye of the storm where fear became faith. There God still waits, the Sun of love piercing the darkness. Fly! Fly with the starlings to safe haven.

❖

The Chinese, so the linguists claim,
make one word serve for two;
both *chance* and *danger* look the same
to Deng and Wong and Wu.

Not being Oriental, Lord,
nor blessed with bravery,
I find that I can ill afford
such opportunity.

With little challenges I'll play
for self-approval's sake,
but save me, Master, from that day
the earth begins to shake.

Amen.

Promise Them Anything

In my straits I called upon the Lord;
    the Lord answered me and set me free.
The Lord is with me; I fear not;
    what can man do against me?
The Lord is with me to help me,
    and I shall look down upon my foes.
It is better to take refuge in the Lord
    than to trust in man.
It is better to take refuge in the Lord
    than to trust in princes.

(Psalm 118:5–9)

Behind the courthouse, plain people standing in respectful silence surrounded the flatbed truck. Their deference extended even to the act of breathing as they allowed the echoing pauses in his speech to serve them as well. They gulped air when he did, scratched when he did, looked up to high heaven when he implored the Greatgodalmighty to rescue these poor sheep, shorn by big business, savaged by special interests.

He said he was plain folks too, but they knew better. There was only one Packard among the muddy machines choking the rutted street, only one white suit in the sea of fading denim, only one voice piercing the late afternoon heat. They hadn't defied the midday sun to finish their chores early or risked the tires on the old Chev or dared to lay claim to the wrong side of the square in order to hear a fellow farmer complain about the weather. They came to make a silent statement at the hoarse request of a "hick from the hollers", as he called himself, who sported a diamond ring as big as a pine cone and promised the same for everyone. They came to see what made him so frightening to old money and new as he raced around the state raising dust and expectations.

Each man and woman knew they would vote for him; they had made up their minds months ago when the newspapers first printed his outrageous notions. Through barely parted lips, they ate his sandwiches and drank his soda pop as he indicted, impeached, and unmanned the incumbent and his hangers-on here in the county. No gnarled hands came together in applause, no cry escaped a wind-wrinkled throat. As for laughing at his barnyard mockery of the local politicos, well, in these tough times, laughter was a precious commodity and the courthouse windows were filled with faces. Theirs was the silence of the lied-to who had heard it all before every four years. Some would allow themselves a nod here and there as he confirmed his country roots with a hard-scrabble story; others sucked in their cheeks at the audacity of a complete reform of state services including a universal old age pension plan, free health clinics, higher farm prices, lower taxes, better highways. They knew he didn't want their applause. He knew he had their votes in his back pocket. What he wanted here and in every sleepy county seat was the presence of a crowd at the back of the courthouse. They obliged him by forsaking the marble steps and the bronze doors where a week before the Sheriff, the Commissioners, and all the foot soldiers accumulated in a twenty-five year incumbency had welcomed the Governor and his State Troopers and their sirens. They obliged him by circling an empty stake truck flanked by road graders and cement mixers. They didn't have to roar their approval to scare the old gang; they just had to be there.

From time to time he fortified himself from a pitcher of what looked like iced tea. Women pursed their lips; they had heard about his escapades in the city. Their husbands had heard the same stories; they licked their lips. Tears came to his eyes as he recounted the poverty of his parents, driven off their land by the same breed of sharpers who loitered on those marble steps. He recovered quickly and told of his rise to prominence as a defender of the poor, turning around lost causes, comforting the afflicted, afflicting the comfortable. After an hour and a half, all concerned had had enough. He closed with a list of every scandalous item the controlled press had printed about his private life. If they couldn't get at his ideas, they would try to get him; he wasn't an angel and didn't pretend to be one. The pitcher was nearly empty; no one accepted the invitation to come up and taste his tea. "They never do", he said. "God is good." A man almost guffawed, but caught himself. He finished it off, wiped his mouth with the back of his hand, and told them not to vote for him but for themselves.

He jumped to the ground and shook a few hands as the crowd quickly melted into the clogged street. They had done their part. Doors slammed, starters whined, a hundred conversations began. Over the crunch of rubber on gravel, they spoke in brief bursts of hope and fear. Of the faces in the windows and who was going to replace them. Of those staring strangers in the crowd and which side they were on. Of better treatment from deputies and assessors. Of paved roads and cleaner contracts and human beings at the bank. Of a new broom at the Capitol and how much that pension plan would cost. Most of all, they talked about the man himself and how down-to-earth he was. No, he wasn't a country boy anymore, but he remembered. That's what he had said again and again: "I remember." Would he, she thought as her gaunt husband got out to shoo the pigs away from the sagging gate, will he . . . remember?

❖

Across our screens they flit, thirty seconds of sincerity, nineteen diagonal inches of patriotism, images crafted in the pollsters' laboratories; we can hardly recall a time when we believed, when we took at face value the promises of those whose only stated ambition was to represent you and me in total dedication to our most altruistic ideals. Face value. What did his face look like before the ministrations of the make-up man? Where does her chic hair style go when the studio air conditioners are shut off? And what do they say about us when the camera is trundled to the next game show or soap opera? We don't know, for the business of self-advertisement is very serious; only a fool would spend that kind of money on a pleasing persona, then risk it by offending someone with an ugly truth. So, voting becomes a game of chance, the tender of a slip of paper with an X on it in the hope that some decision, policy, or program will match the pledges proclaimed so fervently on the hustings. Then, one morning after the swearing-in, we wake up to find the promises have been forgotten. Our latent distrust becomes rueful cynicism. Once again, to our ever-diminishing surprise, we have been misled. What first we learned after the flatbed truck left the courthouse has been confirmed in election after election over these long years: They can not or will not remember.

Although painful, this is a salutary revelation for us who have put too much trust in princes. Despite an impeccable manicure, the jabbing finger on television has no more lasting effect than did the tub-thumping fist on that sweaty summer afternoon in the square. Neither could signal much success in righting wrongs or fulfilling expectations so shamelessly encouraged. Every campaign produced a winner, every winner induced disappointment, that mixture of failed dreams and scepticism best described as world-weariness.

This is not all bad. We are right to be weary of a world that takes human endeavor so seriously that the thought of a higher power and a final judgment plays no part in its schemes. If money is the mother's milk of politics, then unconditional humanism is its animating spirit. The philosophy that says that human beings, left to their own devices, will create the peaceable kingdom here on earth is disproved in the aftermath of every election. Try as they might, even the most honest of our officials cannot escape the power of cold cash, the compromises forced by expedience, the once hidden but now loudly proclaimed agenda of interests inimical to any hint that this world is passing away. The faithful Christian, caught up in the cry for instant gratification, is brought up short by the realization that there is another life, another plan, another world to be won as this one falls to dust. Thus chastened by truth, he falls back on prayer.

The promise of the Author of life can be stated simply: to save from itself this race of incarnate spirits. Nowhere has God promised to perpetuate a system or a nation or even a church past the endtime. Protection for a chosen people, yes. Guidance for the faithful, yes. Lepers cleansed, sight restored, even the dead revivified, yes, yes, yes. But all, devoted supplicants no less than godless empires, eventually fall like brittle leaves in autumn in a world tumbling toward oblivion. It is wise to be world-weary in a world wearing out. Commonsense Christians speak to the One whose design is unchanging and eternal; they know his promise and seek their part in its fulfillment.

If everlasting communion with God is our fulfillment, we begin that intimacy now. While prayer teaches us how far we have to go, how incomplete we are, how blind to God's goodness, how lost without him, it also makes quite obvious the folly of the princes of this world as they cajole and appease the Pollyannas, assuring them that this time it can work, this time peace will break out, crime will be eradicated, cancer will be cured. Prayer whispers that it can't happen as long as the human heart shuts out God. Left to ourselves, and absent the acknowledgment of divine providence, we perish on the rocky shoals of self-redemption.

Prayer reverses our course, puts us in touch with the Other, the Keeper of Promises, who holds a place for us locked in his love. He runs for no position, cannot be bought, will not compromise his plan. He is king and healer of our hearts whether we know it or not. His reign over us only begins in this dispensation; it will come to full flower hereafter. Our task is to know him and the faint stirrings of his kingdom here and now. This is prayer. This is our salvation. This is a weary world's only hope.

Without smugness or condescension, commend to the Father those who have swallowed whole the notion that gain means progress and majority makes right. They need to see the same light that guides you and me, that beacon of hope that shines from a far, far better place upon a world wearing down. We, the people of the promise, recognize that this life is but a stepping stone to eternal fulfillment. May it please God to enlighten our brothers and sisters.

❖

Upon the rooftops
crowning buildings glassed and gilt
lie expectation's refugees,
torn in wing and feather
by the hurricane of promises unkept
swirling round your city, Lord.
Imprisoned in a net of disappointed hopes,
they will not rise again to dare the fickle currents
of temporal achievement.

You came to tell them
parables of sparrows saved,
bucolic tales of soft, still skies
far from urban ferment
where ambition's invitation fills the air
guaranteeing glory now.
Release them, Lord, to enter not the futile flight
but that serenely soaring flock so long awaiting
the kingdom of your making.
Amen.

God Don't Make Junk

Love is patient, love is kind. It is not jealous, [love] is
not pompous, it is not inflated, it is not rude, it does not
seek its own interests, it is not quick-tempered, it does
not brood over injury, it does not rejoice over wrong-
doing but rejoices with the truth. It bears all things,
believes all things, hopes all things, endures all things
(1 Corinthians 13:4–7).

After the first shock, your angry heart squeezed out one
vengeful plan after another. You would wait until the supper dishes were cleared—a cold supper, as cold as your
eyes—and then drop the paper next to his coffee. It would
kind of plop, falling open to the local news section. You
heard his gasp at the accusing photo. But that would be too
dramatic. Bette Davis could get away with it, could even
circle the picture in lipstick . . . that was just it. Should this
be high drama, should it seem to make that much difference to you? Besides, he always glanced at the paper before
he ate.

Better to make a stinging joke of it. Show him how blasé
you were and how much of a riffraff he was for sneaking
around. Cut it out, no, rip it out, put a single thumb tack in
the raggedy corner and stick it to the door. Let it flap there
in the hall, a banner of betrayal. But you weren't ready to
let the other tenants in on your shame. Finally, you settled on the injured party approach; you would pout, but in

a mousey way, Myrna Loy with her hair all stringy from getting the house cleaned up. No kiss, just the folded paper and back to the stove. Since he always scanned the headlines first, you put a check mark under "Shriners' Parade Attracts Thousands", a fittingly sharp dagger pointing to two faces too close together.

That plan unraveled when he didn't come home on time. At 7:16, after riding a rollercoaster of emotions for two hours, you heard him park the truck in the alley. He didn't give his usual whistle, didn't skip up the stairs two at a time: he knew. All your schemes were based on surprise, the evidence thrown in his face, the cheater humbled. You twisted the paper in your hands as he carefully closed the door behind him.

"I suppose you saw the picture. One of the guys at the garage showed it to me when I got in. I can explain if you'll let me."

After a year of marriage he knew the rhythm of your jealousy as well as he knew the rumble of his Diamond-T. It was your right, your duty to race your engine, throw your mind into reverse, spin your wheels in frustration, blow the horn of righteous indignation. He had learned that his job was doggedly to promote logic while you ran him over and spattered him with the mud of past betrayals: the cute dispatcher at the terminal, the Assistant Manager's secretary, both your sisters-in-law, and just about every woman who stocked a bread rack in the stores on his route. This time he mumbled about an old schoolmate who was caught with him in the parade traffic jam. He couldn't move the truck for an hour yesterday afternoon, so he joined the throng and ended up next to Angie Koehlmann as the elephants went by. Photographers like the elephants, and, well. . . .

That day, though, he fell silent well before you ran out of gas. You went on with the program, waiting for his protestations of innocence, waiting for him to tell you he never looked crossways at another woman, anticipating the catch in his voice as he swore on a stack of Bibles, ready for his outstretched arms. It didn't happen. You wound down abruptly, foregoing the description of a faithful wife taken for granted, laboring to turn this one-room, day bed-kitchenette into a home all by yourself, all alone all day long while he toured the city on the make. Instead, between your concluding sobs he said, "You're right. And I was late today because I called Angie after work and we went out for a couple of drinks. We made a date for tomorrow. I'll be late then too." He grabbed the paper, crumpled the offending picture and threw it on the floor. The old rocker yowled as he sat down hard and snapped to the sports section.

You thought of calling your mother. You thought of packing, of stomping out and slamming the door. Mostly, though, you thought of what you had done, forcing him to lie like that. You saw him hanging around the garage after work, afraid to come home because he had seen the photo. "Sick to death" was how he described his feelings after the last dust-up a month ago over his politeness to the super's wife. That one ended with your promise to be reasonable and an embrace that cooled too soon. Now he had had enough, growling that he was going to make your nightmares come true.

How young and foolish and mean you were back then. You wanted more than love, you wanted possession. You went too far and it was a long time until you were sure he hadn't carried out his threat. Those were the cold years when you were merely married but not trusting. For many months after the Angie episode, you were afraid even to ask him how his day had gone. New stores opened, his route lengthened, the boss was replaced; you never knew the details, never shared the adventure of an ailing truck or the pain of a storekeeper's insult. Tersely he reported what he thought you needed to know to allay your suspicions. Cold years, shorn of the silly confidences that keep a marriage young. You both crawled into middle age with relief.

Each on a separate track, you recovered gradually. Your love for one another eventually regained its warmth. You are known now as an ideal couple, gabby, intimate, playful, a husband and wife who can laugh with and at each other. But you never laugh about the beginning, about those years beyond recovery.

❖

Unfounded suspicion in a marriage or any close relationship usually arises because the supposedly injured party feels deficient in some desirable trait. There is indeed a real injury, but it is self-inflicted. A woman who groundlessly suspects her husband of infidelity sees herself lacking that which is necessary to keep him. A man who is overly possessive of his friends fears that they will be snatched away by a more attractive personality. Fruitless are prayers for a permanent, rewarding relationship when you and I doubt the goodness at the core of our own being. We are praying, as actors say, "against type", for we are asking that a friend or mate might cling to us despite, that is, in the face of, our unattractiveness. Such petitions are doomed from the start. Since we don't like ourselves that much, can we really expect God to force someone upon such an unappealing object?

There is only one prayer capable of banking the fires of groundless jealousy: the prayer of trust. First, we must tell God that we trust his power of creation, that we believe firmly that from the Supreme Good can come nothing that is bad. In the grammar of the ghetto, God don't make junk. Our prayer is one of assurance that the spark of the divine shines brightly in us, that God's fingerprints are all over us. Needless to say, this petition must be accompanied by the necessary resolution to rid ourselves of any pretense or shallowness that dims the image of God in us. Second, we pray that the other person may accept our true worth, that his good sense, her power of perception will penetrate the chaff blown up by our foibles and fickleness. Here, we are praying with the grain, for God gave his thinking creatures a special insight for goodness. We trust that, with the aid of grace, they will attend to the value that we cannot see in ourselves.

If the Creator had fashioned even one person on earth to be friendless, all our prayers of trust would be in vain. The witness of his Son belies that suspicion. The scars of a leper, the Magdalen's seven demons, the curses of the crowd at the Cross, none of this ugliness was enough to blind Jesus to the pearl within. He even offered the choicest morsel at his final meal to his betrayer. His whole life was a prayer of trust culminating in his willingness to give his Father his last breath, to commend his spirit to the One who led him through misunderstanding and rejection to Calvary and to fulfillment.

Trust the Father who is leading you through the bleakness of suspicion. Trust the Author of goodness who is calling another to attend to your loving heart. Trust the friend, the spouse who wants to love you as God loves you. Saint Paul says that love and jealousy are incompatible. Live no longer in a house divided. In the serenity of prayer, see your fears for what they are, doubts about yourself, not the other. Make the plea of the worried father in Mark's Gospel your own: Lord, I believe in myself, help my unbelief.

❖

Reaching
    from the edge of nothingness
    to molten core of earth,
    you formed a layered universe
        of basalt, loam, and atmosphere
        and twenty million miles from here
        a lonely molecule each year
            until creation fit
                the limits of your love.

Trusting,
    Lord, your constant providence,
    I ask again a proof
    that one unlucky sliver rimmed
        by salty sea and Everest
        did not escape your grace and rest
        apart forgotten dark unblessed,
            a pall about the earth,
                a race stretched thin and cold.
                Amen.

Modern Times

Jesus said to them, "A prophet is not without honor except in his native place and among his own kin and in his own house." So he was not able to perform any mighty deed there, apart from curing a few sick people by laying his hands on them. He was amazed at their lack of faith. He went around to the villages in the vicinity teaching (Mark 6:4–6).

When the strip wagon got away from the kid, you laughed with all the others. The twenty-foot by twelve-inch ribbons from the rolling mill were still slippery after the galvanizing process; all a wagon boy had to do was pull the front wheels too sharply to the left or right, and the shimmering steel slithered in all directions over the littered floor. Stools overturned, tool boxes emptied, operators danced away despite their safety toes.

A new wagon boy, a couple of weeks of spills before he quit or got fired were welcome relief from the incessant pounding of the stamping machines. So you went along, not maliciously as some of the old-timers who loved to see a kid choke up and get watery-eyed, but for the simple alteration of things, air going through your lungs in a different way, a chorus of guffaws competing with the pandemonium of the plant; you laughed to encourage the silvery strips to make wondrous, snakelike patterns as they coiled and eddied across the greasy concrete. In laughter and sparkling metal you forgot for a moment how mean and gray was this job.

Once you had been a wagon boy providing comedy for other men. You had turned corners too quickly and loosed the bright cascade. But somehow you got a handle on the job, chose a certain cart each morning, one that you knew, that you could trust; you neither quit nor were fired but pulled your load for a year, longer than anyone could remember. And were promoted, your fondest dream realized, to be an operator, to manage a stamping machine with all its lights and levers. You would turn out your quota and more, every day a thousand perfectly formed electrical connector boxes, each with five perfectly joined sides and six perfectly round holes and twelve perfectly punched detents, all squeezed out of flat steel by two tons of hydraulic force pumping up and down six times a minute. This was your product, an open-front box, four by six by three inches, into which electricians in some upscale subdivision would poke freshly cut wires and place a switch to bring light to milady's mirror. How many had you made? Roughly two million over the years. And which one broke the secret that you and the machine had changed places? It didn't happen like that. The truth seeped in through the cracks in the concrete, ending with the realization that Hi-Press #03176 was your boss, calling you to stab the buttons and clear the safety gate and stomp the treadle. You fed it on signal, cleaned its mess after a jammed cycle, emptied its finish bin. You moved only when it said so. When it didn't, when a storm cut the power, when a strike silenced the plant, you became inoperable, unnecessary.

Silly things happened at home. During a Sunday afternoon barbeque, you spied Marge giggling with a neighbor, staring at your approach to grilling hamburgers. You checked yourself, discovered your movements locked in ninety-degree angles, a robot flipping hamburgers at the sound of the buzzer, stepping mechanically back and up, kicking a treadle that wasn't there. Often in the car you turned the key, hit the ignition and saw your hand reaching under the dash to remove the preceding man's last box. One morning you stumbled into the kitchen rubbing sleep out of your eyes, then rushed to pull Marge's head out of the oven, spilling Easy-Off all over the floor. When you started in about the safety gate, she broke into tears. It wasn't a laughing matter any longer. You called in sick that day, spent the morning at the table talking it over. There was only one solution.

But there were no comparable jobs. You watched your workmates more closely, saw them back away from their machines, waiting for material, moving slightly to the secret rhythm of their momentarily silent masters, afraid of losing the beat, of stepping back to the power switch out of sync, of being repaid with a crunch of metal and flesh. You were not ignorant of the price of inattention: with luck, just a finger. Hot pain for a while soothed later by the disability check. Would it be so bad, really? Marge would have to get a job. You could go into life insurance like Art Martinez who paid double for his ticket out last year, pinky and ring. Of course, you loathed salesmen and couldn't stand pain and Marge had a weak constitution. So it was thirty years to retirement, six million more perfect boxes, a lifetime of jerky dreams. . . . Until the night the kids wanted to watch a Chaplin festival on television. It was *Modern Times* and Charlie started to tighten those bolts.

They didn't laugh at first, never having seen a wagon boy over twenty-two, much less one with salt-and-pepper hair. The shop steward was moving quickly among them, tersely explaining that while you would be getting tops for your task category, it was still barely half of an operator's pay. So maybe it was pity in their sidelong glances, the same thing the department manager was trying to hide in his downcast eyes last Friday when you laid your cards on the table. He said it was highly unusual; you said the union rules allowed it as long as there was an opening and you signed a paper saying it was permanent to protect seniority. He couldn't find a paper like that and the steward had gone home; you would sign after work today.

They looked at you openly now, staring around the clanking presses, moving their eyes up and down with the safety gates, stepping up to the treadles, stepping back. You had spent the first hour this morning picking out just the right wagon. It pulled like a dream, responding precisely to the lightest touch. You would still be the best wagon boy this plant had ever seen. You were the operator of a fully loaded machine that would never have a mind of its own. In the middle of the shop you stopped behind a pillar and jerked the front wheels sharply to the left, unleashing a gleaming stream of steel against the presses. You covered your grin with all ten fingers as the whole crew roared. They needed it.

Modern times are stressful times and much of modern prayer revolves around the desire to overcome or at least live with stress. The numbing repetition of the assembly line, the glaring impudence of the computer screen, the unending demands of housework and children, all the major and minor aggravations of contemporary society combine to squeeze the sweetness and civility from life. Too often the Christian comes to prayer not in answer to a gentle call, but in exhaustion, falling to his knees empty of words, filled only with churning frustration. Little wonder that a harried breadwinner experiences aridity in meditation. The petition simply to endure another day is frequently the cry of a strangled soul seeking to achieve that which God himself cannot accomplish.

Since the presumption that God is on our side has led more than a few to despair, it might be wise in times of stress to forego a plea to overcome or understand or endure in favor of a blunt request for the courage to step back *permanently*. A brief respite with God before plunging again into the pressure cooker may not be the prescription of the divine Physician. He could be calling you to remove yourself for good from a certain sector of the battlefield. So radical a step does take courage and discernment in a society that places such a high value on personal achievement at every level. Even the most well-intentioned can, to the detriment of their spiritual health, equate the approval of spouses, children, friends, and employers with that of God himself. Sometimes the best way to discern God's plan is to stop doing what drives you to distraction, if only to honor the truism that distracted people can't hear God.

Jesus' departure from Nazareth is a good example of a wise man stepping back from a frustrating situation. "He was not able to perform any mighty deed there", so he went around to other villages. Note the difference between this episode and others where he retreated to a quiet place of prayer to refresh himself before reentering the fray. The Gospels do not report a return to his home town. It was not a place where he could be successful. If Jesus was sensible enough to acknowledge that his powers were overmatched by the challenge, shouldn't we, whose powers are so meager in comparison, emulate his common sense?

Jesus achieved much in his public ministry, but there were times when even the Son of God had to admit that discretion was the better part of valor. You and I have been called to follow in his footsteps, to cultivate the field our Father has sown and now and then to take part in the harvest. Our mission, however, is circumscribed by human frailty and defined by God's plan. The refusal to admit our limitations is as foolish as the refusal to take the time to discern the divine will. The prayer of stepping back is a healthy remedy for both kinds of foolishness.

Take time today to assess your chances of success in a particularly stressful area of your life. Count your blessings, your talents, and your shortcomings. In the presence of the All Powerful admit your weakness. He may be asking you to leave this part of the arena for an indefinite period, perhaps forever. This departure could be the most courageous thing you'll ever do, far more difficult than bowing to the expectations of family and friends by forcing yourself once more into a no-win situation. Seek God's design. Trust in his wisdom. Believe in the rightness of his son's departure from Nazareth. Step back, and if it be God's will, stay back.

❖

The Principle of Doctor Pete
is not to turn ambitious feet
toward situations rife with dread
where God and angels fear to tread.

If self-conceit sends out the call
to bang hot head against brick wall,
persuade me, Lord, to step aside
and in your reasoned peace abide.

Since there were places you passed by
and causes lost, not worth a try,
point out to this still fervent soul
a more inviting, simpler goal.
　　　　Amen.

The Great Separation

At once the Spirit drove [Jesus] out into the desert, and he remained in the desert for forty days, tempted by Satan. He was among wild beasts, and the angels ministered to him (Mark 1:12–13).

Nearly every Saturday for two years now, you and the boy had climbed to the ridge on the old Indian trail. You were always grateful that he ran well ahead; separation offered the opportunity to pant and wheeze in a most unexemplary fashion. He could have been up and over and down to that day's lookout before you were halfway to the crest, yet his habit was to dawdle beside the path near the top so that you could both hurry through the last of the wind-twisted trees together and catch the same first glimpse of the dam. Here, you would exchange terse observations on the more obvious signs of progress. Your real work began farther down the waiting slope at a spot he would choose, a log or outcropping seemingly picked at random in his head-long descent. Even with arms and legs flailing, even when you thought he would give in to gravity and like a tumble-weed roll to the roaring river, he was scouting for a new perch—each one a bit lower than the week before—from which to share with you the fascinating details of what it took for man and machine to tame a river.

That was later, however. Back when it all began, nothing you could say would persuade him to leave the ridge-line. For months, you went down alone, calling him like a puppy, assuring him that the steep trail was safe. He stood above in the wind, babbling in awe, pointing to this giant derrick, that naked turbine, waiting for you to come puffing back. Though he never said it, something dark in your own memory told you that the trail had nothing to do with his hesitation. It was the sheer size of the dam, the massive bulk of concrete, the soaring arches, the brooding towers. He was too small to take it all in, too frail to stand up against it, afraid of falling under its spell. This supposition was confirmed when the dam was topped off, when it stopped growing and he didn't. In the second year, he was at least two inches taller and wider, took pride and comfort in his growth, and began the weekly helter-skelter down the slope, daring the colossus to reach for him, fall on him, envelop him, always in control, coolly sighting in his rampage the point below which he could not safely pass. There he would wait until you carefully made your way down to compare notes on each new development. Until this day.

In the car on the way to the trail, he had talked excitedly about the dedication. Two months from now, Mom would pack a lunch and the three of you would drive around the mountain to picnic at the site where the President would give a speech and press a lever. In deference to you, he called him "that man in the White House", but without your sarcasm. He would learn soon enough which way the country was going. Someday you would have to sit him down and tell him the facts of life about creeping socialism. But that could wait until the dam was finished. No use spoiling a project you both had put so much into.

Two months more: you hated to see it end. Merv and Turk, whose boys were seniors, said it was bound to come with the first fuzz on the lip. "That's when 'Yes, sir' stops and sass begins." There had been fine down under his nose for half a year now and still you were pals. It was these hikes that kept it going. This day his descent was unusually heedless as if he were trying to prove a point, to push beyond the limit. Suddenly, something tripped him, pulled him down, batted him like a bear toying with a rolled up woodchuck; he bounced toward the river as you got your feet going. Before you took a second step, one of the blighted pines on the precipice stopped him.

You scrambled down, skinning elbow and knee; he was on his stomach, shaking like a chihuahua. You rotated his arms, made him bend his legs. Nothing was broken, but his shivering pointed to shock. He had to get out of the sudden chill that had come upon the slope. Your repeated assurances that he was okay didn't seem to do the trick. Was it his neck? He would not move his head, would not look up. You shielded your eyes, tried to find the sun. Then you knew.

No sun, no clouds, no sky. You were completely engulfed in the shadow of the dam looming over you. You felt it now, the memory of a boy whose friends went right up to the tangled wreckage of a car towed to the police garage the night before. How many killed? Three? Four? They stuck their curious heads through the smashed windshield, sniffing for death. You stood back, near the office. You couldn't get any closer to the tortured metal, the charred tires. It was too big for you, too violent, too powerful, a twisted totem whose menacing judgment you could not control.

He wouldn't rise, wouldn't even get on his hands and knees. You touched him, found soothing words, but they were unconvincing, betraying your ambivalence. He crawled back up the slope on his belly, silent, hugging the sharp rocks without a whimper. You stumbled beside him, more certain with each step that this was the last time. He got up on all fours as you passed the level even with the top of the dam. On the ridge he stood for a moment in the clawing wind, then without looking back, walked stiffly down to the car and got into the back seat. The rearview mirror revealed nostrils flared in self-disgust, jaws clenched against a sob, and in between, that smudge of manhood aborning. There were no tears; there would be none. The great separation had begun; no more dawdling to let you catch up. As you put the car into gear, you saw how it would be the next time: a moonlit night, some grudging father's overloaded Ford parked in that hulking shadow, a bunch of guys from the basketball team straining for laughter over the moaning turbines.

❖

There comes a time in the bittersweet career known as parenting when prayer is the only meaningful contact possible with our children. It is the period of *sturm und drang*, that long, heartbreaking war that begins when a mortified adolescent gives his mother her last kiss in church and may end when a young lady gets her first full-time job. In between, the ships pass in the night bound for school, sports, parties, for any port not populated with parents. Sullen silences, bizarre behavior, fiery arguments signal a battle within, that protean conflict between individuality and dependence. There, we cannot go. We vainly pour the balm of our own experience over the cauterizing sting of common sense, but the soul of youth is too deep, we are told; no adult, much less a mother or a father, could possibly understand.

But we can understand, for we have been there, have faced the judgment of peers, parents, and self. Some of our own wounds may not be healed yet, but at least we have learned enough to name the beast: that daily test of will, wiles, dimension, and doubt against the brooding, intractable powers-that-be. What you and I are today is the fire-tried product of a thousand verdicts rendered upon our adolescent yearnings for self-identity. Yet for all of that, for all the hard-won wisdom we could impart, we cannot make ourselves heard above the din of today's battle.

So we do the only thing we know how to do. We pray. We pray not for mundane triumphs, not for good grades or better friends or best in show. This is a battle for the soul, not for social development. Now, long after our narrow escape into adulthood, we pray that these orphans in the storm may survive the irrational yet compelling convergence of external judgment and self-estimation that nearly did us in. We join our proffered love to the infinite compassion of Christ and ask that it may envelop the gangling boy who will not make the team, the gawky girl who will not be accepted by her classmates. We remind Jesus of those forty days in the desert when his own sense of identity was tested against what the Tempter offered as the world's more logical valuation. There loomed the mountain of empire, the parapet of public adulation. He did not allow expedience to fall upon him or cynicism to engulf him. He was blessed with the solace of ministering angels and emerged with his personality, his mission, his dream intact. Most of us emerged from our deserts pretty much intact thanks to ministering angels, family members who prayed us through our dance with the wild beasts.

Your prayer for your hapless children goes right to the heart. It pierces pouting lips and angry ears to rest with God's guidance in the deepest caverns of the soul. There, a new life is forming, a whole person capable of right judgment in the face of so many conflicting opinions. The more constant your petition, the greater the chance for the kind of growth that withstands failure and success as well. How long will it take? How long did it take you? When you

think of giving up, remember who you are and that you
know who you are because someone never stopped praying sense and solace into you. Given the life that hangs in
the balance, prayer is, in every sense of the word, the best
you can do.

❖

Protect them not
from windmills spoiling for a fight,
ambition's fraudulent perfume,
or callow dreams
    of wrong submitting speedily to right,
for wisdom burnished in the fray
shall crown the knitted brow of youth one day
    as pruning spurs the bloom.

Protect instead
these introspective hellions, Lord,
from hearing in some madcap test
the knell of hopelessness,
    that self-condemnatory chord
confusing worth and victory.
Bestow anew your gift of dignity
    despite the errant quest.
            Amen.

They Drive by Night

Let mutual love continue. Do not neglect hospitality, for through it some have unknowingly entertained angels. Be mindful of prisoners as if sharing their imprisonment, and of the ill-treated as of yourselves, for you also are in the body (Hebrews 13:1–3).

Officer Friendly he wasn't. Under the hooded slicker his face was hard, defying the pelting rain. Rain was against the rules, and he was regulation from tightly knotted tie to gleaming boots that threw back the lightning. You too were against the rules in this overloaded truck with expired plates and no running lights. When he asked to see your three-axle permit, you knew this ill-starred odyssey was over. You played for time, fumbling for what you didn't have—perhaps a few more drops of sweat running down your back would change your license from private to commercial—and wondered if small town judges really had books on their rostrums to throw at luckless pilgrims lost in the night.

It wasn't supposed to be this way. The plan was for you to run only in broad daylight on well-traveled roads. Your brother-in-law, who, when pressed, admitted that his old International wasn't quite up to state specs, swore up and down that highway cops didn't bother anyone who went the speed limit. "And this baby can go." Barry was right. It did go, but at the first gas station, it didn't stop so well. You could still see that attendant vaulting a trash barrel as you passed the pumps and plowed into a convenient pile of old tires. Unknown to you, the plan had begun to unravel well before that. Supposedly right behind with the girls, Betty finally pulled in a half hour later. Little Deborah, never a good traveler, had had an accident before her mother could get the station wagon stopped. Worrying over the fading brakes, you hadn't even noticed their absence from the rear view mirror. Well, it was easier to clean a car seat than fix a master cylinder on a ten-ton truck. After the mechanic had finished howling over the pump man's leap for life, he said he would have you going in about an hour. About six hours and forty dollars later, you eased back behind the giant wheel. Betty and the girls had gone ahead this time, all of them angry at not being missed when they had to stop. Now you would see them if anything went wrong. Since the mechanic had warned of weight inspectors prowling the main highway, you and she agreed, rather icily, on a road barely perceptible on the map. That was four hours ago, the first of twelve times you had been told the truck would be ready to go "in a minute". Why hadn't Betty backtracked? This was no time to be spiteful.

You thought you caught a glimpse of a pearl-handled revolver as he reached for his flashlight, the better to reveal the full horror of your crime. The offending license slipped easily out of your nearly empty wallet. Two lonely ten spots, a reminder that nobody had to talk you into saving money. The moving companies you called quoted prices frighteningly close to the down payment on the new house. Betty's farmer brother wasn't going to haul cattle this weekend. He and a couple of his hands would help you load; the real estate agent had promised his sons on the other end. It all went well until you mounted to the running board. The truck was too high, too wide, too independent. Your feet barely touched the pedals. You had to move off the seat to engage the stiff clutch. But you smiled, waved at the kids, kissed Francine from next door, and ripped a limb from her prized oak as you backed into the street. Francine clenched her fists but the roar of the engine muffled her words.

You survived the morning by standing on the brakes. This baby could go all right, but at speed it took two hands to steer and two feet to stop. You held fear at arm's length by thinking of your new life in the Capital, a job in which at last you would be appreciated. You rehearsed the advantages for the girls: better schools, those beautiful parks; their tears would be forgotten soon enough. And you counted again all the money you were saving; just gas for this clattering behemoth—500 miles, seventy-five gallons, only $22.50 give or take. Barry wouldn't want anything for retrieving his baby next Friday. He was a fan of the pennant-bound Sox; you'd treat him to a game. Gas! There was a station ahead. You jammed the brake pedal. A friendly attendant waved you toward the pumps. At first, he was smiling.

Now it was eleven-thirty at night. You had finished the story of your life, or at least that part designed to elicit sympathy from General Patton who sat stonily beside you in the cab. Surely he understood that you meant no harm. Your only motive was to save some hard-earned cash. He opened the book of the dead: no running lights, expired plates, no commercial driver's license. "Flat feet, dandruff, several bad habits", you mumbled. He didn't laugh. It came to $175.00. He was also the Justice of the Peace and would take a check. Your present balance, $35.00, leapt from the speedometer. No, this would not be the time to bounce one. "I'll have to take you in. Follow me." You stepped on the starter as he opened the door. "No, leave her here. Get into the cruiser."

On the way, he made it clear that tonight you would be an official guest of the township. You could use the phone tomorrow to make arrangements for the money. "I don't get many stopovers. They usually have a check. Only two ever floated on me and both times I went to get them, triple and travel." Thank God you hadn't tried it. "They think small-town folks are stupid, but they got another think a' comin'."

You didn't want to beg, but anxiety over the safety of your family overpowered pride. "No, you can call tomorrow. I haven't got time to escort prisoners to telephones. I've got to get back on patrol." The village limits sign was splashed with mud. Somethingville. Pop. 320. The only light on the two-block main street hung over the door of the city hall, a house that looked much like the one you had left forever this morning.

You were concentrating so hard on Betty's notorious lack of nighttime driving skills that the station wagon at first seemed like a dirty joke your mind was playing. Dirty it was from the mud she had gotten stuck in on the shoulder when Debby again gave up to the forces of nature. You found that out later. Now, all you heard was his laconic report of spotting them walking back to town about 7:00 p.m. He had pulled them out, found the gas tank damaged by the struggle, and pushed them back here to wait for you. When you asked how he knew you would stop, he pointed to the siren that had blasted you off the road. "Y'know, I waited over three hours for you. I think I'm gonna add my time to your fine." He cracked what you assumed stood for a grin and motioned you out of the car. "We've always got the upstairs bedroom ready. I'll be back at one. Don't wake up my better half. There's eats in the fridge."

❖

If your habit is to meditate in the morning hours, consider an exception just this once in favor of sisters and brothers forced to drive by night. Prayer is indeed timeless, entering into a realm swept by God's own eye; yesterday, today, tonight, and every tomorrow are one in the steady gaze of the Mercy. But make this meditation when darkness has gripped the earth firmly so that you may benefit from the look of things unseen, the shadowy specters just beyond the weak beam of tired headlights. Tonight, offer your prayers on behalf of the nomads of the road.

Outside your black windows, a mile or two away on the bypass skirting the city, rumble the rusty vans and crammed sedans of the dispossessed. These are not the exiles permanently burrowed into the utility tunnels beneath Grand Central Station. As recently as a week ago, or was it a month, these weary travelers had, if not roots, at least a place to go when the sun went down. Oh, it wasn't much, a rent-subsidized flat or a room with her folks, but it provided that all-important address for the employment forms. Then something happened—part-time workers were laid off, the state supplement ran out, a fight with the in-laws—something that splintered the fragile construct of subsistence. Suddenly, a neighbor was offering ten bucks for gas and some clothesline to keep the trunk closed. Rumors of work in a far-off city, perhaps even the thin promise of a job: hope traced out on an oil-stained map. It all happened so quickly. Now in the darkness, worn-out tires and tired-out children whine around your town, your home, your warm and dry and solid place.

It is not easy to pray for folks we've never seen. We need a face, a name to hold up to God. Most of all, we need some matching experience, a feeling of shared struggle to call forth a compassionate petition for those separated from us not just by a mile of darkness, but by a life of luckless wandering. Most of us have always been able to mark an X on the map. "That's where we'll be staying tonight. We've got reservations." We go from one spot to another and always end up at home. We are not in flight; we are en route. What is that bond, that common contest that will link our prayers with the souls of those out on the bypass fleeing from nothing into the unknown?

That bond is called life. Settled or searching, well-off or worn-out, we have all come from nothing to be pilgrims bound for glory or Gehenna. Each of us has traversed bleak landscapes, unsure despite our faith of reaching that house of many dwelling places. We have known the valley of darkness, the rough and lonely road illuminated only fitfully by hope gone aglimmering. If we need a face, a name to hold up to God, only a mirror is necessary, for in accepting ourselves as rootless pilgrims, we commend all the road-weary to divine guidance. In your warm room behind the fragile pane, pray not, "There, but for the grace of God. . . ." Rather, see your face behind the slapping wipers, see your children huddled on the back seat. Our journeys differ only in degree. We all drive by night, straining to see beyond our own lights, praying that what is unseen will not bring us to grief, hoping that at the end of the highway we shall find our reservations confirmed.

❖

Full house:
> he beaming rubbed his hands in satisfaction
>> so pleased to repeat the sound most roundly
> to rounded wife and dusty husband.

No room:
> he turned to soothe a fussy scribe's impatience
>> then stopped to behold again the woman
> so much in need of soonest shelter.

In back:
    he tersely gave a servant girl instructions
        assuming that here the matter ended
    without disturbing well-born patrons.

A boy:
    he shambled to the stable in the morning
        obliged to bestow the landlord's blessing
    but found just footprints leading southward.

Dear Lord:
    assign to me your most remorseful angel
        that innkeeper peering out the window
    when strangers at my gate seek haven.
                Amen.

My God, My God,
Why Have You Forsaken Me?

For he has not spurned nor disdained
    the wretched man in his misery,
Nor did he turn his face away from him,
    but when he cried out to him, he heard him.

(Psalm 22:25)

The hot breath of the lead bull pressed heavily upon your bare back. How far behind you had fallen. Not merely a straggler anymore, you were dead last, just a hoofbeat away from being trampled into Pamplona's cobblestones. Ahead, one of the bunched runners turned to glimpse the impending carnage. It was the Old Man himself, Papa Hemingway, eager to take it all in, savoring a new scene for his next book. The crowd, scenting blood, roared its encouragement, not for you but for *el Toro*. Your legs gave way; the shrieking from the sidewalks shattered the silence of the room. You jerked your head up from the desk and stared at the moist imprint of your cheek on page 258 of *Modern English Literature: Analysis and Comment*. The Baby Ben said 2:25 a.m. Who was screeching like that? Maybe the strain of finals had pushed someone over the edge. The dorm echoed with the cry, a wail rising and falling like a . . . like a siren.

From the top bunk, Andy mumbled about crazies pulling false alarms; there had already been three during grind week. The sound of running feet drew you back to lush Navarre and your race with death . . . wisps of smoke streaming from Papa's bobbing pipe . . . wisps of smoke snaking in under the door. . . . . Andy's bulk thudding on the floor made you sit bolt upright. "Don't open it. Touch it. See if it's hot." It wasn't, but an acrid, brown haze filled the hall as students ran for the stairwell. You grabbed your wallet, Andy grabbed his pants. You weren't afraid until you passed the garbage chute. Its iron door had turned dull red; smoke pulsed from around the frame. Did that mean the lower floors were on fire? Your cautious pause at the banister lasted only a millisecond; the herd carried you down the steps past three more trash chutes, all glowing and spitting, but nothing worse. A garbage fire. And tonight of all nights. What next? You were never good at cramming, but at least it helped to have a room and a desk and a book.

From across the street, it was rather spectacular. Flames shot from the roof vent forty or fifty feet straight up, narrow, slender, your childhood image of the pillar of fire in Exodus. The firemen knew their stuff. Only a few scaled the ladders to the roof; the others pulled hoses inside the lobby and up the stairs, opened those sizzling doors and called for water. The pumper trucks roared sixty miles an hour standing still. After fifteen minutes, the men began to come out with their helmets off. Thank God they were so efficient. Most of you were milling around in your shorts, doing gym stunts to counter the January chill. You were about to learn how lengthy a fire clean-up could be.

It took two more hours before the dorm counselors were allowed to call everybody in, two hours of wind sprints and sarcasm forced from chattering teeth. The story came piecemeal. Mope Ratliff on the top floor had finally driven his neighbors up the wall with his yodeling. At the midnight break, a couple of them invited the Mope out for a burger while others raided the scrap paper bin in the basement. Kentucky's favorite son returned to find his room filled from top to bottom with crushed newspaper. He stopped yodeling, favored all and sundry with a rich sampling of mountain-man blasphemy, then shanghaied some hapless freshmen to make a million trips between his door and the chute. Later, somebody loitering in a lower hall probably saw a counselor coming and had to rid himself quickly of a lighted butt.

First dawn brought uncertain shadows and the realization that D. H. Lawrence was making no more sense than James Joyce. Chesterton was boring, Maugham pointless, and Eliot seemed to end everything with a whimper. What had these pale and powdery Brits to do with real life anyway? Hemingway. There was a man who wrote plain English. He'd make it short and sweet. Real life was pizza with the boys and a pitcher of beer at the Donkey and Heather Toomey in Poly Sci. Ah, sweet Heather of the moors. But Papa knew the other side too, the sour taste of hopelessness. Real life was 9:00 a.m. in a twenty-tiered exam hall sitting on a sticky seat. Real life was a headache from the smoke still hanging in your room. Real life was flunking it, a core course, and doing it all over again next year.

Maybe Halvorsen, the dorm's resident agnostic, was right after all. Maybe God was perverse, jiggling this and that, making the Mope yodel, setting in motion a series of events that would end in your humiliation, your punishment for . . . for what? goofing off all semester? not putting a foot in church since September? making Heather cry? all of the above? Maybe that's what Joyce was talking about: one day, just one, filled with seemingly trivial choices and minor mistakes that in reality were the whims of an Almighty bent on teaching you a lesson. *Something* must have gotten into you yesterday, a mysterious force keeping you from cracking a book until after supper, telling you a morning swim was just the ticket to make your mind more supple, persuading you to spend three hours buried in *The Sun Also Rises* to recapture your zest for the challenge, ordering you to visit Heather way over at Delta Gamma because she got honors in Lit, even whispering that a prolonged argument with Andy would sharpen your wits. Who fed you all this irrational crapola? Since the last thing you wanted was to muff the exam, common sense pointed in only one direction. It had to be God, sitting up there with his model railroad, bending that rail, shorting out this crossing sign. He wanted a smashup, designed a detailed timetable for you, a schedule of wasted hours and yodeling and sirens to route you straight through to disaster.

You slammed the book shut and Andy rolled over. So be it. Can't fight city hall. If you failed, it was an act of God. You had done your best to overcome his tricks. "Lazy and lustful." That's what you said in your last confession, two years ago or more and the words still bright as a neon sign in your mind. Well, who made you that way? And who started the fire? And who gave you what must be a migraine? And who pushed paper and pencil under the pointy noses of all those snobby Englishmen in the first place? It wasn't your fault. You set the alarm for a quarter to nine, got off a few reassuring curses at the chirping birds, and fell into bed with your sneakers on.

❖

Much of what passes for prayer is really thinly disguised accusation. My petition for a less turbulent relationship with certain co-workers too often hides the presumption that, for some reason, God is pinching off the milk of human kindness. If he would only open the flow, peace would reign. Your plea for relief from the numbing persistence of a common cold hints that a decision to go coatless to the store one day last week involved a perverse intervention from above. Such impiety springs from a combination of what the psychologists call projection, that tendency to attribute to others the faults we see in ourselves, and the fact that God is an easy target. The absolute Other, because of the barrier of several dimensions of space and time, is able least to defend himself. My confrere at the next desk has little hesitation in telling me I'm the bad apple in the shipping department. Your wife at the kitchen table says "I told you so" immediately after your first sneeze. The Almighty, the Creator and Sustainer, the King of Kings and Lord of Lords, can't fight back; he is a ripely indictable co-conspirator in our troubles. Indeed, being all-powerful, he is often assigned all the blame.

This accusatory thread running through what seem the most humble of prayers is hard to deal with because it is part of the dark myth that nurtured those of us brought up with the Just Judge. Reinforced by Old Testament images of divine anger, the picture of a menacing God cowing and manipulating the chosen people rivets our attention, distracting us from the merciful ministry of Jesus, the wounded healer. We may even entertain the idea that the carpenter's son is engaging in a public relations effort, a studied program of high-visibility compassion and forgiveness, in order to mask the stern Father's frown. Now and then the mask slips. Look at that poor fig tree, the man with the millstone around his neck, and how about those innocent pigs doing cartwheels off the cliff?

The problem with accusatory prayer is threefold. First, it distorts the authentic portrait of God made plain when Holy Scripture is contemplated in its entirety. Granted, the Old Testament contains many primitive sketches of Yahweh doling out or withholding his favors. At times, he seems to turn his love off and on like water out of a faucet. When the Lord says in Leviticus 26:12, "I will be your God, and you will be my people", we get the impression that the *and* really means *if*. Leviticus, as other books of the Pentateuch, is replete with threats of punishment for faithlessness. However, a more generous sampling of Scripture reveals that God remains faithful no matter what his people do, constantly renewing the Covenant in the face of their betrayal until it receives its ultimate configuration in Jesus Christ. Praying to a God who measures his love contradicts the central theme of the Paschal Mystery: in Christ, all are called by infinite love from their sins to new life. This wondrous fulfillment of the constant promises of the Old and New Testaments cannot be the gift of a fickle, arbitrary, and vengeful lover.

Second, prayer that makes God responsible for our failures denies an essential human faculty: free will. If he is to be reproached, even in the smallest degree, for friction at my workplace or your underdressed bravado in the snow storm, then our absolute freedom to decide is compromised. A pattern of prayer based on the suspicion that God is behind our misfortunes quickly leads to the death of hope; our feeble attempts to choose righteousness, our agonized strivings for self-discipline are doomed in the face of divine opposition. Again, a panoramic reading of Scripture disproves such dark imaginings. From Abraham to Jeremiah to Mary, a call goes out, a call to choose. Each of these, and all the other heroes and heroines of our spiritual ancestry, exercised the power of decision, that gift given by God to enable us to select him, among all the forces of the universe, to be our Master. To say otherwise, to pray to a God who restricts our freedom, to ask him to remove his heavy hand, to cease his Machiavellian interference in our lives, is to court despair. One day we shall take a long look at the God who toys with us and shudder at the thought of living with such a monster for eternity.

Third, making God the fall guy releases me from the responsibilities of spiritual growth and Christian witness. Oh, I'll try to play the good soldier for Christ, but my heart won't be in it. Since God will make his own disposition of whatever challenges confront me, I won't go looking for troubling encounters. Prayer then becomes an exercise in shallow breathing, an escape from all endeavor for the common good. As the peaceful kingdom will only be advanced by divine edict, both individual and mutual efforts are futile. Living turns to waiting; prayer counts the days. Once more, Scripture says it isn't so. Moses says it isn't so as he leads his people to freedom. David says it isn't so as he whirls the sling above his head. The brothers Maccabee say it isn't so as they cleanse their homeland of foreign rule. In the Acts of the Apostles, we see yet more assuring evidence of the vitality of the partnership of God with men: the burgeoning of the Church through the inspired enterprise of the followers of the Way. All of this started in the Garden, not with sin, but with love, constant and life-giving on the one hand, faltering and fearful on the other, but Love called to love and that call endured through every page of the Bible and is still heard today, a call to act despite misgivings, to believe in the face of doubt; it is a call heard most clearly in the praying heart of a person convinced that the very being of God is love.

In your prayer, accuse God of nothing but love. Meditate on the many kindnesses of Jesus in the Gospels. They far outweigh his sharp yet salutary warnings. Look at the human face of God at the intersection of those two rough-hewn beams. Convince yourself of the constancy of divine affection by turning to Psalm 22 and the words Jesus uttered as he died for you, but read it straight through. Hear the Savior's echo of mankind's uncertainty at the beginning and his celebration of triumphant love at the end. Here is nothing less than the alpha and omega of prayer.

❖

Once more 'mid tumbled dreams I kneel, my God,
and wonder
if your affection
fluctuates
according to the ebb
and flow of my belief.

Unsure of motives jumbled in the moil
of living,
and contemplating
outcomes bleak,
I let suspicion strain
the friendship you desire.

Renew my faith long humbled in the fray,
assure me
of love unmeasured,
turn my doubt
to trust in you alone,
my efforts to your will.
Amen.

Lemonade

[Jesus] summoned the twelve and gave them power and authority over all demons and to cure diseases, and he sent them to proclaim the kingdom of God and to heal [the sick]. He said to them, "Take nothing for the journey, neither walking stick, nor sack, nor food, nor money, and let no one take a second tunic. Whatever house you enter, stay there and leave from there" (Luke 9:1–4).

It was the odor of the Sunset Motor Court that finally won you over to the idea of a trailer. Pungent autumn bonfires, the essence of the forest clinging to the Christmas tree, the delicate perfume of violets newsprung from the shivering soil, none of these, nor any of the other aromas of a year come full circle could mask that mixture of mildew and decaying dreams that had permeated your very pores during those two nights the previous July when you learned what hell would smell like. That was the bitter end of your first vacation trip without the kids. Your other stops had been with politely resigned relatives; you couldn't impose upon them two years in a row, couldn't relax under those faintly disapproving gazes. But neither would you subject yourself to the clammy embrace of a string of peeling clapboard cabins. The drumming agony of three hundred miles a day over the euphemistically labeled "improved roads" of the Midwest deserved sweeter solace than imprisonment within moldy walls teeming with uninhibited life. So it was either his plan or no trip at all. You very much wanted to see what you missed last year: that little church made of broken bottles in Iowa, those hillbilly villages in Arkansas. What you didn't want was ever to smell another Sunset. In the end, your nose won out. Your brain, you decided later, had not even been in the running.

Your education began the day he brought it home. You had assumed a trailer was something like a wheeled zeppelin with silver sides containing three-quarter-sized chairs, bed, sink, refrigerator, and all the rest, a cute mobile doll house in which you two would bump into each other and laugh. Hadn't you seen caravans of these land yachts sailing down the new concrete highways? Well, Charlie Schmidt down at the shop stood against that kind of luxury. He liked to rough it, and anyone who was privileged to borrow his trailer had to get along with the bare necessities. That was the gist of your shamefaced husband's report after he towed into the driveway what looked like the wagon the newsboy pulled behind his bicycle. Oh, you both joked a bit at first. Yes, he should have asked more questions when Charlie rhapsodized about the open road and independence, but, after all, it wasn't the Sunset Motor Court or Aunt Milly's sun porch.

What it was, was flat, no higher than the fat-bellied trunk of your old Nash. "That's for speed on the highway." It had tiny, solid rubber tires, not pneumatics. "That's for protection against blowouts." It had a lot of canvas. "That's to make it light so we can get up the Ozarks." And it had a crank. As he whirled it vigorously, up rose what could only be called a tent, a tent on top of a Radio Flyer. He dived inside and began to unfold things: army stools, a tin table, a cordless hot plate. He called you over as he strung one of the hammocks fore and aft. He wanted approval, but you just stared through the isinglass window at the hooks. Everything was on hooks—pots, pans, lantern, water bag, an ax, fishing gear, hip boots, even a cloth wardrobe, for your party dresses, no doubt. A turn of the crank and it all came up like a castle in a child's pop-out book. You were not hooked.

"No," you growled, "I'll call Aunt Milly." The "But Hon's" started. He had a lot of reasons, some were good, but good or not, they all ended with, "It won't be so bad." Not comforting at all. You pictured yourself next Tuesday night in some ravine in Missouri with coyotes or whatever sticking their noses under that tent flap. But you needed proof; the weight of the evidence had to be heavily on your side or it would be a summer thick with recrimination, so you gave in to his final suggestion. When the kids came home from the beach, you would drop them at your mother's and go out to the old quarry for a trial night, a "breakdown cruise", he called it. You shuddered.

Mom was her usual long-suffering self, but she brightened considerably after he had gone back to the car and you whispered that she probably wouldn't have to take them next week. "I don't think we'll be going on a trip this year." At the quarry, everything combined to fulfill your prophecies. The arid summer had left a green scum over the shallow water in the pit, an incubator for a million flies that promptly found the openings in the canvas. They were not deterred by the rain that fell from the driest skies in a decade. He couldn't get the Sterno open until he went to the car and grabbed the ice chipper out of the glove compartment, thereby knocking the match box into a puddle. The can opened easily then, while you vainly searched for extra matches in Charlie's tackle box. You found, instead, the fish hooks, or they found you. Luckily, you weren't a bleeder. The sandwiches, though, were good; he didn't complain about your lack of trust in making them. No matches meant no lantern, so you placed the flashlight—again, evidence of your lack of faith—on the corrugated floor and talked around yawning silences, swigging sweet, warm lemonade from mason jars. As the batteries wore out so did your appeal to the flies; perhaps they found no more unbitten patches of flesh. In the failing light, you hurriedly hung the hammocks and jumped in fully clothed. He jumped too hard and the pole at his head surrendered. The hollow knock of his skull on the wheelwell made you giggle and made him mad enough to spin you to the floor. You pulled the hammocks over you as coverlets and laughed until your sides ached, rehearsing the whole awful affair until the rain stopped and the moon poured through the cool canvas. Was it self-preservation that made you turn to your honeymoon: the missed train, that fleabag hotel, the walk around the little lake in the misty dawn? When you had nothing, anything seemed a luxury. He recalled a feeling that you had forgotten long ago, the halo of freedom, of being alone together for the first time, three days in a new world where neither of you were known, accountable only to each other and to your love. You threw back the flaps to look at the stars in the newly washed sky, your stars, just as bright as they were then. "You must remember this, a kiss is still a kiss." He still couldn't sing, but your private lullaby never sounded so good. You turned away from the stars, toward each other.

The next morning, your usually stoic mother showed uncharacteristic disappointment when you announced that she would, after all, have the kids starting Friday night. When the week was over and down through the years, you both called it the best vacation ever, that time when you packed a tiny trailer, stopped for extra matches, mosquito repellent, a bag of lemons, plenty of sugar, and went not to Iowa or Missouri or Arkansas, but back to the old quarry.

❖

Many prayers are barely disguised complaints about the imperfection of the status quo. This irritating health problem, that abrading relationship, those financial worries are lifted up to the Almighty in the hope that he will tinker a bit here, twist an arm there, and move the process with compassionate haste to a reasonable solution, that is, one that fits our idea of justice. In these petitions, we believe we stand solidly with the fiery prophets of old who seldom failed to call Yahweh's attention to the shortcomings of the chosen people. Often, the consummation devoutly to be wished was a rain of brimstone upon the heads of the errant. How this would move them toward perfection is left to conjecture. Since we are often unsure whether the fault lies in us or in others, we are more circumspect, calling for a series of subtle adjustments that will end in the greatest good with the least pain for yours truly. We want neither bloody revolution nor the reconfiguration of the galaxy, just a reasonable change for the better. The pitcher loosing the 0-2 pitch would call it a prayer for an easy out.

The New Testament doesn't offer many easy outs. Again and again, Jesus tells his disciples that they must thrust themselves into difficult situations seemingly impossible to master. In our Scripture passage from Luke, he even mandates hardships for his followers when he sends them out on mission with only the bare necessities. They are to leave behind apparent essentials like food and money. While his purpose is to teach them dependence on God alone, they also learn to make the best of a bad bargain. They return bubbling over with news of the successful use of his name. "Even the demons are subject to us" (Luke 10:17). Good news, indeed, but not to be overlooked is the fact that they returned at all. They didn't starve, they didn't get lost, they didn't want for hospitality; they turned difficult situations into opportunities ripe for the working of God's will.

In prayer, try to keep from complaining. Instead, go to God with a mature view of conditions, human and divine. He, from whom all good things come, is not torturing you; he is sending you where you are needed most. What pleases him is the exercise of your ingenuity to extricate yourself from today's quicksand and reform it into fertile soil. Even if the problems he calls you to face are of your own making, you have the God-given power to solve them. What honors God is not resignation to the will of an egocentric world or to your own weaknesses, but a prayer of confidence that he will work through the faculties he bestowed on you. In other words, you were designed for this day of tribulation; ask your Creator's help in working out that design.

Saint Irenaeus said that God's glory is man fully alive. It is hard to tell if a man is alive when the hammock is gently rocking to a sweet summer breeze. When the bough breaks, then insight, wit, invention, understanding, and courage come into play; the whole person comes alive. Our prayer should be that we might have the common sense to exercise all the strengths God has given us, and even to use the frailties inherent in our humanity, to give him glory. God is scarcely magnified by resignation to the status quo, nor is he much exalted by complaining about it. He is honored most by human beings becoming ever more perfectly human. Like that most perfect One of all among us, he who seemed to discover every single place in Israel where angels feared to tread, we bring our knowledge of ourselves and our trust in God to the barricades. That combination is called Christian confidence. The prayer of the confident Christian is not for a basket of bitter fruit, but if life lobs lemons at you, pray that you remember the recipe for lemonade.

❖

They sought a second tunic
> when wintry fingers roughly probed
> your shy disciples' coddled faith
> unused to icy strife.

I need this robe of reason
> against the chill of circumstance,
> surprise encounters reaching in
> to freeze my tepid life.

You kept their coats, stern Master,
> lest self-protection substitute
> for faith's invigorating fire,
> and comfort hobble zeal.

Now take my cloak, Lord Jesus,
> and loose in me that ardent pulse,
> your Spirit warming, answering
> this frigid world's appeal.
> > Amen.

And Then Do with Me What Thou Wilt

As they led him away they took hold of a certain Simon, a Cyrenian, who was coming in from the country; and after laying the cross on him, they made him carry it behind Jesus. A large crowd of people followed Jesus, including many women who mourned and lamented him. Jesus turned to them and said, "Daughters of Jerusalem, do not weep for me; weep instead for yourselves and for your children" (Luke 23:26–28).

> We adore Thee, O Christ, and praise Thee.
> Because by Thy holy cross Thou hast
> redeemed the world.

So began the oddly lilting dirge, that chant of self-accusation you sang each Friday night during Lent. Saint Alphonsus Liguori had managed to lay bare the convoluted secrets of your deepest soul, had applied the righteous X-ray of his insight to the hidden path you had traveled since the preceding Easter, had found you out and presented this bill of indictment to the Court. You stood at the dock and heard your sins enumerated as they were heaped upon the bleeding shoulders of the innocent Christ. The evidence was overwhelming:

> It was not Pilate, no, it was my sins that
> condemned Thee to die.
> It is not the weight of the cross, but of

> my sins which has made Thee suffer so
> much pain.

You knew nothing of this obscure Alphonse, but he certainly had you pegged. And what of his extrascriptural knowledge about details of Jesus' torment unknown even to the Evangelists? The Bible said nothing about Jesus falling on the way to Calvary, nothing of Veronica's miraculous towel. But Alphonsus Liguori knew that when Jesus and Mary looked at each other "their looks became as so many arrows to wound those hearts which loved each other so tenderly", and he knew that when the soldiers stripped Jesus of his garments "they dragged them off so roughly that the skin came with them". Little wonder he was able to convict you of sins you had been only dimly aware of—thoughtless neglect, pusillanimous pride—that accumulated to become on those Friday nights the crushing burden borne by the Crucified One.

> How many times Thou hast pardoned me, and
> how many times have I fallen again and
> begun again to offend Thee.

In the whirlwind of jeers and catcalls that buffeted the stumbling Jesus, you heard each of the brave curses you had hurled at your enemies. In the blows that rained upon his head, you saw your wrath coming down upon some innocent who crossed your path. The sticky-fingered Judas was the model for your petty thievery. The Apostles who fled blazed a trail for your escapes from church attendance. You and the dragooned Simon from Cyrene were kindred spirits when it came to volunteering a helping hand. Saint Alphonsus read you like a book, chapter by ignominious chapter, verse by infamous verse.

Well before the Twelfth Station, the strait jacket of guilt had squeezed the breath out of you. Your gasping soul took its deserved place in Hieronymus Bosch's hell, ready to be numbered among the satans and satyrs who ground hardened hearts into fine dust and fed it to each other. Betrayal was ashes on your tongue.

> I weep for the offenses I have committed
> against Thee, because of the pains which
> they have deserved, and still more
> because of the displeasure which they
> have caused Thee who has loved me so much.

Why would anyone subject himself to this weekly recital of shame? To be sure, Lent was a time of purification. Blame for the sufferings of the tortured Christ must be laid at the feet of the sinner, but enough was enough. More than once you left the church in the grip of a fierce headache after "they then closed the tomb and all withdrew". Were you a masochist? Did you welcome this painful remorse? No, what brought you back each week was not the rehearsal of your offenses against the Lamb of God. You returned because of the tiny miracles that Saint Alphonsus had managed by art and faith to hide in these fourteen forlorn scenes. In the middle of the blood and grime of despair, the loving Liguori secreted here and there a bright promise of immortality, a glistening, golden nugget called *hope*. The "Stations of the Cross According to the Method of Saint Alphonsus Liguori" were about the miracle of hope.

> I beseech Thee, by the merits of this
> sorrowful journey, to assist my soul in its
> journey toward eternity.
> Give me the necessary helps to persevere
> in Thy grace until death.
> Permit me to love Thee, for I wish but

Thee and nothing more.
Make me rise glorious with Thee at the
    Last Day.

A heart made brittle by a lifetime of bad habits had
to be broken open by sorrow before healing balm could
be poured into it. Your stony soul had to soften before
it could receive the impression of God's forgiveness. Perfunctory examinations of conscience routinely failed to
convince you of your guilt. Month by month, your skin
grew thicker, scales hardened upon your eyes. Since your
sense of regret was barely perceptible, your ability to see
any promise in your world waned. You became a shallow
breather, expecting nothing, risking no disappointment.

Then Lent would come around again. Saint Alphonsus
would throw your sins in your face, make you recoil at the
results of your folly: a crown of thorns, mockery and spit-
tle, a fall and another and a third, and always the slow arc
of the mallet. Yet, in the most unexpected places, he offered to eyes veiled in sorrow a bright pinpoint of gold,
a spark of hope—the Master's perseverance in doing his
Father's will, his tender love for his horrified mother, and
especially, his forgiveness of a common thief.

Hope is still a rare commodity, more so today because
we rather glibly talk ourselves out of sin. Mesmerized by
pseudopsychological explanations for our moral outrages,
we stumble through life like sleepwalkers in a minefield,
unmoved by the evil exploding all around us. Since none of
it is our fault, we have no need for repentance. And because
we will not take the blame for our transgressions, because
we see no necessity for the Lord's forgiveness, we are bereft
of hope.

The Stations of the Cross are monuments to hope. Each
indignity that Jesus endured came from the hand and heart

of another being. Saint Alphonsus asked us to see ourselves in Christ's tormentors—raising my hand in anger, constricting your heart in hatred—and then to stop and meditate on the gift of forgiveness. Perhaps his language is too florid for our age, his estimation of the worth of men too dark, but his theme still echoes with truth: we are sinners in need of God's forgiveness. And forgiveness is our only hope.

❖

In the post-Christian era, what many people call prayer is really an exercise in self-improvement. That which used to be sin is now an accident of circumstance. Freud and his disciples tramp into the mists of personal history, even invading the womb to prove their theories of moral relativity. This gene, that dream, those traumas of childhood are the sources of our misadventures. Mistakes merely breed mistakes, and no one is culpable. You don't need the gnarled hand of a priest signing absolution; you need stroking by Doctor Feelgood.

Sadly neglected is the prayer for a more realistic sense of sin. Yet it is precisely the loss of, or better, the flight from, moral responsibility that has plunged this age into hopelessness. Oh, we hope. We hope to improve our standard of living. We hope for peace in the world, for our children to succeed, for security in the golden years, but we never have to hope for God's forgiveness because so many savants, secular and sanctified, have told us it isn't necessary. Don't bother the Almighty with regret over your mistakes; he has more important fish to fry, like Idi Amin and Charles Manson.

Unless Christians wish to confine their hopes to what is seen, they cannot afford to expunge sin from the language of living. If we are convinced that Christ's Resurrection means personal redemption, that he gave his life to save us from our sins, then we must admit our sins in order to have any kind of fruitful relationship with him. Did he die only to offer the possibility of salvation to a category of evil-doers delimited by ogres like Adolf Hitler and Jim Jones? Are our offenses so minuscule that we are cut out of the loop? We know better.

Jesus sacrificed all because you lied to your husband and I turned away a beggar from the door. Your husband was never the wiser, my beggar got a handout on the next street, but both of us offended humanity and humanity's God. We pray, then, for forgiveness. We tore the seamless garment of divine love, and only Mercy incarnate can mend it. This is our faith, that God's plan can be repaired by his pardon. We pray for forgiveness so that our hopes, like the eagle released from captivity, can break free from the earth and soar again.

❖

Against the rolling thunder,
above the jeers and catcalls,
        did they hear you
        pronounce the benediction
                in accents thick with Galilee,
        forgiving them because
                they knew not what they did?

Against the knell of commerce,
above the breaking story,
        do we hear you
        announce the hope of sinners,
                a word for all humanity,
        forgiving us who know
                exactly what we did?

Good Jesus, pierce our deafness
with blessed absolution,
   whispered mercy,
   compassion for unheeding
      disciples loath to lend an ear
until the deed is done
     and rue is our reward.
    Amen.

Every Second Wednesday

You are an enclosed garden, my sister, my bride,
    an enclosed garden, a fountain sealed.
You are a park that puts forth pomegranates,
    with all choice fruits;
Nard and saffron, calamus and cinnamon,
    with all kinds of incense;
Myrrh and aloes,
    with all the finest spices.

(Song of Songs 4:12–14)

The attic said Aunt Pet. Everything in it was square with the world: all trunks and boxes piled in pyramids, winter coats from left to right by size in the chiffarobe, lantern, ladder, and carpet beater on hooks, the dress form modestly draped, magazines stacked according to date. Even the floor was swept, the exiled furniture dusted. Well, she had all the time in the world, up until last Saturday anyway.

The funeral had been neat and austere, just the family, a few of her piano students, and the members of Polyphony, her music appreciation club. Only one organ piece, carefully chosen by the ladies she met with twice a month, graced the ceremony. No incense, no straining choir, on her instructions. Nor would she be plumped and padded for viewing. The stern, gray casket was closed. After seventy-two well-ordered years, Pet was not about to make of herself an object of emotion.

As her favorite niece, you had charge of putting the house right for showing. Not that there was any work to do. The first thing you ever remember her saying was, "Live each day as if it were your last." She was always ready for the lightning bolt, the careening bus, or as it turned out, the massive heart attack. Did she fall on the porch so that the ambulance attendants wouldn't track mud on her carpet?

Now, before the real estate agent arrived, you were looking for something, an album, some letters, anything to tell you who Miss Perpetua Ann Cosgrove really was. The designation "favorite niece" had entitled you to nothing more than an infrequent Sunday afternoon in the parlor. She would make the tea; no need for you to get up, no need for you to bring curious eyes into any other room. Just satisfy her with slightly exaggerated tales of life in the suburbs a world away from this white clapboard cottage on Maple Street. While you rattled on about Little League and barbeques, she listened intently, eager to learn of exotic amusements and the chaos of family life. She didn't have a car and took no newspaper. You suspected that your call announcing a visit gave the telephone its only exercise. She braved the madness of the street once a week, quickly purchasing the necessaries, taking her short list and sensible shoes to three or four neighborhood stores. A fellow member of Polyphony picked her up on each second and fourth Tuesday for the meetings. On the way to the cemetery, as Mrs. Deschler confided that Pet always sat in the back seat in case of a crash, you remembered another of her maxims: "One can't be too careful."

It was in an old piano bench under a yellowed sheaf of Chopin etudes: a quarto volume bound in cordovan with a tiny key in the burnished lock. Were she still downstairs perched on the edge of the wing chair, you would not have hesitated. She would never know. Now that she knew all, you felt the piercing gaze. But hadn't she left it to be opened? Why else would the key be here and not hidden in a sachet on her dressing table? The lock turned with a delicate click.

Gold-tipped pages, unlined. Scarlet silk ribbon marking the last entry fourteen years ago on a day late in April. "Mattie [would that be Matilda Deschler?] on funeral. Small congregation. Most hymns not up to the Club's standards, but floral arrangements adequate. I may not write again. It is too painful or perhaps too confining. The more of him I put on paper, the more the mystery slips away. Like a novel, when I finish, I know it all. I don't want to lock him up, control him that way. O God, help me, help me."

She must have written more, but thought better of it. Several succeeding pages were neatly cut close to the binding leaving the last third of the thick book blank. You sat at the top of the attic stairs and started from the beginning. It was not a daily diary; most of the entries were about a month apart. He was a sheet music salesman from downstate, a widower of three years when they met at a concert the day after her forty-sixth birthday. He had come to the house two weeks later, then visited with her nearly every second Wednesday for the next twelve years. They spoke about Saint-Saëns, Debussy, and loneliness. His wife had died of cancer. They had no children. Her reportage was matter-of-fact, Aunt Pet on paper. The weather. His new suits. The solitary life. His presentations at the Club now that the ladies had made him their sole supplier of music. Favorite writers. The endless war. Sunday's program from the Met. Illness. Conversations in a darkened parlor.

Each of these dry-as-dust recitals was followed by a commentary seemingly written by someone else. The hand was the same, the ink, the abbreviations, but the Aunt Pet you knew, she with the bun pulled tight behind her head, couldn't possibly have done them. Oh, she could have copied the florid lines from the Rubaiyat, the precise yearnings of Emily Dickenson, the holy passion of the Song of Songs; you had seen the sources on the shelf over the mantel. But where did Pet learn the language of desire that cried out in her own words from so many of these pages? "J.", as she called him, had touched the romantic in her, had opened her lonely heart to the half-forgotten music of youth and called forth from the darkness of inhibition ardent songs, tender poems, pledges of confidence and self-giving. Again and again she sang of the beauty of life, the pain of love. Although many among these pages too were removed, those that remained to conclude an entry always bore the stamp of thankfulness, a prayer of gratitude to God for sending "my J." to her.

Strange—or was it?—that the missing pages did not intrigue you. Nothing, not even her own admission in black and white, could convince you that this chaste, devout woman had ever led her J. out of the parlor. If the diary had been intact, if therein lay descriptions of earthly passion rivaling Boccaccio, you would have seen them as the inevitable unfolding of the dreams she lived with from one visit to the next. Pet was still Pet. She had plied her scissors so that you, her literary legatee, would not get the wrong idea. "Don't tempt good boys", she would say as she closed the garden gate when the Maple Street Raiders played ball in the alley. She just wanted someone to know. Not all of it, but enough of it.

Your concentration was so intense, your scan so rapid that you didn't notice your tears until they began to blot the final pages describing his brief battle with an unnamed disease. You had to wipe your eyes to see the next to the last entry. "Mattie called about J. The Club will go down for the funeral. I can't." The front door was rattling. You locked the diary and put it in your purse, then went to the octagonal window at the end of the attic. The little key fell among an arpeggio of daffodils in the center of the garden.

❖

Above all else, the Bible is a book of love. When first we settle down with it, seeking inspiration for our daily meditation, the essence of God's tender affection may escape us. We cannot help giving immediate attention to royal intrigues, angelic choirs, ritual curses, oracular utterances . . . all the coloratura extravagance of grand opera. Yet, every page of Scripture contains a secret song, an incredible admission of the Creator's gentle passion for his creatures. Beneath the sweep of adventure and the clash of traditions, the truth is heard by those who cultivate a serene sensitivity to God's word: he cannot get enough of us. We monopolize his thought. We fascinate him much more than he interests us. While we go about our daily business, the book is still there, the story of the persistent suitor following us, anticipating our needs, yearning for some sign of reciprocal attraction. God dotes on us, a lovesick swain caressing the picture of the fickle maid. Even in our betrayals, we cannot escape his concern. Stubbornly self-deceived in the desert, bowing down to idols, washing our hands of the truth, yes, even killing our brother—and he is there loving without limit, incapable of disinterest.

That God courts his people is not the half of it. As we dip below the surface of the narrative, dismissing as products of their time inconsistent lineages and mythic victories to wonder at the love poured out upon this remnant, that flock, those tribes, as our confidence grows with the realization that we are the people chosen for salvation, each of us is drawn to a still deeper level, the level of personhood

123

where there is revealed the most astounding truth of all. God loves me, the individual, the student, the blind man, the leper, the librarian, the banker, the math teacher, the husband, the child, the woman at the well, the woman at the wall, the thief on the right and the thief on the left. His passion for the solitary soul is so powerful that he enfleshes his affection, sending Jonathan to David, Timothy to Paul, Sarah to Abraham, Joseph to Mary, your spouse to you, my friend to me, and to that maiden lady at the piano—that one over there sitting in her dark parlor, alone on her forty-sixth birthday—a balding sheet music salesman in need of gentle conversation.

It is the experience of the specificity of God's love that the Evangelicals seem to have a lock on with their unsettling question: "Have you accepted Jesus as your *personal* Savior?" Those of us who are growing accustomed to a Church called the people of God are sometimes annoyed by what we see in other denominations as an overemphasis on the individual. We counter with the jargon of community: "There are no solo flights to heaven. We are saved as a people or not at all." But slogans at either end of the spectrum tend to delimit the truth rather than define it. The people of God are individuals with names, noses, and the need to see divine providence as something more than a transcendent concern for the common welfare. We yearn to know God's love on a daily basis, in a form we can understand. Of course, we believe in the specific locus of love that was Jesus of Nazareth. We believe he is still among us intensely present in the Eucharist, but we strain to see him at the office and the bowling alley. And there he is in one of his many manifestations as a caring friend, God's love in the everyday, just as real, just as tangible as Aaron was to Moses and Mark to Peter. We are indeed saved as a community of believers, but we give thanks that some in that community are friends, co-redeemers in league with Love himself to tenderly coax you and me as individuals to salvation.

As you close the Holy Book for today, make your prayer one of gratitude for all the friends who populate its pages. They are the beginning of a long line stretching into your life, the spiritual forebears of those few who stand with you and support you as guarantors, in their finitude and failings, of the absolutely essential truth that you, personally, are the specific object of an infinite love.

❖

I try, dear Lord,
to compass in my straitened heart
the grandeur of your love outpoured;
but where to start?

I cry, dear Lord,
despairing of a life this thin
until you signal hope restored:
a friend drops in.

I sigh, dear Lord,
relieved to know my theme so blue
will touch a most responsive chord;
he speaks for you.
   Amen.

Black and White

Then they brought to [Jesus] a demoniac who was blind and mute. He cured the mute person so that he could speak and see. All the crowd was astounded, and said, "Could this perhaps be the Son of David?" But when the Pharisees heard this, they said, "This man drives out demons only by the power of Beelzebul, the prince of demons." But he knew what they were thinking and said to them, "Every kingdom divided against itself will be laid waste, and no town or house divided against itself will stand. And if Satan drives out Satan, he is divided against himself; how, then, will his kingdom stand? And if I drive out demons by Beelzebul, by whom do your own people drive them out? Therefore they will be your judges. But if it is by the Spirit of God that I drive out demons, then the kingdom of God has come upon you. How can anyone enter a strong man's house and steal his property, unless he first ties up the strong man? Then he can plunder his house. Whoever is not with me is against me, and whoever does not gather with me scatters" (Matthew 12:22–30).

Gable and Garbo and Bogart. A Yankee-Doodle-Dandy marching in jerky rhythm. Astaire and Rogers, Grant and Colbert. Tracy and Hepburn battling to a clinch. You sat in the dark while a bright ray from behind splashed upon the screen now a street in Rio, now an airport in Casablanca, now a caravan of flivvers fleeing heartbreak for California.

And all bathed in the hues God ordained, the natural colors of spies and lounge lizards, mobsters and molls, art deco living rooms and flimsy biplanes, battleships and boardrooms—all in glorious black and white.

Plots mirrored the telescoped spectrum. Boy meets, kisses, marries girl. Cop spots, catches, jails crook. Honor triumphs over venality. Wars are won by the force of personal courage. Love conquers all. We went to the movies because we believed in them. They reflected what most of us considered reality. Oh, there was a seamy side to life, but if it showed up in the movies, it glimmered only briefly like a dead fish on the shore and then was washed away by a tide of righteousness. That's the way it should be, we thought then. That's the way it is, black and white.

Today, we are drawn to those old movies when they are shown at revival houses or on television. Perhaps now we notice that the plots don't make much sense and the dialogue is stilted, yet we are still fascinated as long-dead actors do exactly what we know they'll do. Their predictability on celluloid reflects the predictability of the lives we led when those actors were living legends. We miss that certainty.

If you were growing up back then, you knew exactly what would happen if you came home later than the time specified. You knew what would happen if you talked in class. You knew what would happen if you attempted to take liberties on a date. If you were a wage earner, you knew what would happen if you argued with the boss. If you were a lawbreaker, you knew what would happen if you got caught. To act against custom, law, or moral standards was to step beyond the limits of mercy. Discussion or appeal availed you nothing. Among the many advantages of such an orderly system was that feeling of security called peace of mind.

Take your favorite movie theater as an example. You bought your ticket from a booth projecting onto the sidewalk. The cashier had no fear of a hammer-wielding thief smashing the glass to snatch the change drawer. You didn't suffer from the multiscreen syndrome. There was only one feature at one time. You found your seat, the lights went down, and two things didn't happen. Twenty people didn't come tramping in late to ruin the cartoon for you, and the people around you didn't continue the conversations begun in their living rooms. Most extraordinary was the omission of the warning label at the beginning of the feature. There was no language to burn your ears or scenes to make you blush. Everything was nonthreatening, predictable, designed to make you comfortable, to put your mind at ease. With your popcorn in your lap and the darkened theater holding you in its lap, you saw the world in black and white, much like the scene Matthew painted in our opening Scripture passage. In a world of good and evil, Jesus says, "Whoever is not with me is against me", then makes it clear that he and God are on the same side. Fans of old war movies know how important it is to have God on one's side. The crew of that damaged B-17 consisted of an Iowa farm boy, a New York Jew, a smart-talking Brooklynite, a funny Hispanic, a drawling Alabamian, a scared teenager called "Frisco", and God. The prediction? They would land safely.

Those old movies and the order they reflected look awfully inviting in our unpredictable world. Today, each individual rides pell-mell on a horse of a different hue. Emotions, passions, causes, and protests, splashed with a riot of colors, carry us from one extreme to another, while each person says he is on the right side. What conviction do the feminist, the peace marcher, the union member, the abortionist, the mother of seven, and the Kiwanian share? They are sure that God is on their side. Why? Because they have good intentions. The ostensible aim of each is the common weal. There are no Peter Lorres or Edward G. Robinsons any more. No one plans evil. If evil occurs, it is peripheral to the grand result: the raise, the election, the convenience, the promotion. Those of us who still believe that ends, no matter how popular, do not justify questionable means are caught in a crisis of discernment. Where is God's design among all these conflicting scenarios? What is our role in advancing the kingdom of God?

In confronting the confusion of modern morality, the Christian cannot be blamed for heaving a sigh over absolutes that seem to have gone with the wind. The world will not stand for much nostalgia, however; it calls us back to the present, reminding us that here is where we live, here among mixed motives and clouded outcomes. Grateful for the brief escape afforded by our favorite old movie, we turn again to a scene that is anything but black and white. Fade-out on a kiss? Not today. Today is another tangled reel of film waiting to be unsnarled.

As well as providing abundant solace, prayer arising from remembrance may pose a very real danger. Once the demons of distraction are calmed, the recollection of personal history can take on a stark absoluteness quite foreign to the past event as originally experienced. Memory, like an old movie, is an ardent simplifier. The praying person must be careful to pray *today* for *today* rather than slip into a reverie of a world that never was. Praying with memory means using remembrance as a springboard, not a hammock.

In scripturally based prayer, a simple remedy for "black

and white fever" is to take the roles of various people in a Gospel scene. In the passage from Saint Matthew, was the return of sight and speech the only concern of the possessed man? Perhaps he also thought of the stress involved in reentering the community. "All the crowd was astounded." Were some envious too? Or frightened? The Pharisees were abuzz with cunning, busily trying to entrap Jesus. Didn't even one of them guess what Jesus would say in answer to their questions? How many of these zealous prosecutors sensed in Jesus' answers a wisdom that was powerfully attractive? What of Jesus? "Whoever is not with me is against me." You can't be more absolute than that. Yet another Gospel reports Jesus as saying in a similar setting, "Whoever is not against us is for us" (Mark 9:40). Much more tolerance there. Role-playing the Scriptures forces us to complicate things, to bring the jumble of our intentions, fears, and hopes—the colors of life—into the drama. In turn, the biblical scene becomes more relevant to a world that abhors absolutes.

Only when the reminiscence, be it scriptural or personal, is splashed with living color can the praying person begin to seek meaning for today. As Christians, we believe in absolutes. Prayer is the discernment of Truth with a capital "T", but that search must take place in real time. To seek the truth in a black and white past is futile. When the spectrum of remembrance is so severely limited, little is learned; the lesson won't stretch to encompass all the shades of opinion and choice with which we are confronted every day. Take pains to make your memory work *for* you in prayer. Don't let it fool you into thinking that black and white solutions will fit a technicolor world.

❖

Jesus bar-Joseph, come into my world.
    Beyond the black and white
        chapter and verse
    I offer you a yellow bird
        in a green tree
    against a blue sky.
Walk with me
    to the other side of the mountain
        away
            alone
                apart from scribes and elders
                    demanding yes or no.

See there
    the evanescent mists of dawn,
        a wadi filling with water,
    footprints disappearing in the windblown sand.

Let time and change and yearning
    sweep over us, you and me,
    tumble us upon the living earth,
    shake the coins from our belts,
    scatter gold and silver upon a patch of clay.
See them gleam and beckon in the sun.
    Just once, feel their pull and power to bedazzle.

Soon, my brother, you must return
    to engage the dour doctors,
    those silhouettes of sobriety
        with their stoutly knotted measuring cords.
    They will make your step careful,
                your words colorless,
                  your life a minefield.

Stay, then, a moment more with me in motley
 before you don the field gray of no man's land.
Put your eye to the Father's kaleidoscope
 of maybe and almost and someday,
and rejoice in the riot of wonder
 here behind the mountain.
  Amen.

The Good Mother

Standing by the cross of Jesus were his mother and his
mother's sister, Mary the wife of Clopas, and Mary of
Magdala. When Jesus saw his mother and the disciple
there whom he loved, he said to his mother, "Woman,
behold your son." Then he said to the disciple, "Behold, your mother." And from that hour the disciple
took her into his home (John 19:25–27).

"It's due Monday."
"What Monday?"
"This Monday."
She looked down at her Cream of Wheat while you
pulled the details out of the part between her tightly bound
braids. A religion project. Assigned the second week of
school, due the day before the Immaculate Conception.
This Monday. Had to be something about Mary.

"How about an album, a scrapbook of pictures of Mary?
You could do that in three days."

"I've already got a project. Sister approved it in September."

September. She thought she had plenty of time. First
came cheerleader tryouts. Then football season. Then she
forgot. Anyway, it was too late now. She could never finish
it in time. It meant an F for the semester.

"You never got an F in anything, and you're not going
to start now, especially in religion. You're staying in this
house until it's finished. You've got all weekend. And you
can forget about that party at Sherry's tomorrow."

The Cream of Wheat lost its hypnotic power. She looked up with brimming eyes.

"Aw, Mom, what's the use? It's too late. I don't even know how to start it."

"Nonsense. What in the world is it?"

She mumbled into the Cream of Wheat.

"What? Get your hair out of that bowl, young lady, and look at me. Look at me. What is your project?"

"A grotto."

"A grotto?"

"The grotto at Lourdes. Sister said it was the best project anybody had picked."

Well, that wouldn't be so bad. You could get some clay while you were shopping and she could start in after school. Just a hill with a cave.

"It's got to fit her statue of Mary, the one in class."

She rose and held her hands about a foot apart. It would be too big for clay. Maybe some sand sprayed with something to make it hold together. She backed away when you pulled the ruler out of the junk drawer. She hadn't been rapped on the knuckles since she was little.

"Don't worry, honey, I only want you to put this in your book bag and measure that statue. Get the exact height and write it down. We'll ask Dad to help when he comes home. Many hands make short work. And just to be on the safe side, you better make a visit at lunch period today. Ask the Blessed Virgin to give us some ideas. After all, it's her grotto."

Ed didn't like to be paged on the floor; he was gruff on the phone. But he heard the panic in your voice and said he'd think about it, think about the foot high statue which had grown to twenty-nine inches by the time Trish got home from school. It would have to be a mountain to accommodate such a large figure, but a mountain of what?

Trish was whimpering, still stung by your sharp words of reproach concerning her ability to estimate height. Twenty-nine inches! Was she sure? She *would* get that F if Dad didn't come up with something.

Dad came up with a roll of chicken wire fencing, six cartons of old newspapers from the store, and a bucket of glue. It took him four trips to get everything into the basement, then he opened the *Catholic Encyclopedia*, volume L, to see what the real thing looked like. He couldn't miss the bowling tournament tonight; with Augie out, they needed him. He would get it started, then finish in the morning. In the afternoon, you and Trish could start applying the papier-mâché. By Sunday after dinner, it would be dry and she could paint it.

"I did this once in high school. I think it was a Halloween mask or something. Same process, bigger order."

Trish sat on the steps watching. Things went well at first. A couple of sawhorses held a broad, smooth piece of plywood left over from closing in the back porch. On this sturdy base, he began to nail some scrap wood to hold up the chicken wire. Then things didn't go so well. The wood was old and brittle, given to splitting. The wire was springy, contrary, resisted being formed over the spindly supports. Trish came red-faced into the kitchen. It was obvious that Dad wanted to work alone. She got her first phone call of the evening. The noise from the basement made it hard to guess who was on the other end; it better not be that Freddy Lambert. There was a crash. Trish hung up quickly, stood for a moment listening to words boys said when they got the wind knocked out of them on the field. You told her to go over to your sister's and eat there, then switched on the radio to full volume.

At six-thirty, you turned off Perry Como and went to the stairs, telling Ed he would miss the tournament. He stomped past you, brandishing his thumb wrapped in a bloody rag.

"You think I can get this into a bowling ball?"

While he rummaged in the cabinet for some gauze, you moved slowly down the steps. The ceiling light shone bleakly on a twisted mass of wire and wood, a wobbly Golgotha pierced by a dozen splintered crosses. Serious damage had been done here, and not just to wood and metal. Ed came to the top of the stairs.

"I'm going to the lanes anyway. At least I can watch. I'll grab a bite there. And don't worry any more about that thing. We can't do it. I can't do it. I'll write a note for her on Monday. Don't wait up."

In the morning, he went back down, shutting the door tightly behind him. At your request, Trish had stayed over with Margaret. You hoped she wouldn't return while those animal noises issued from the basement. They brought back the memory of a movie that had scared you silly, *The Thing*. Was Ed fighting the "Thing" down there? He came up just before noon and said it was your turn. You went down, averting your eyes, concentrating on the steps. Finally, you had to look. It seemed to have grown. Sheer size always threatened you, and you stepped back from this grotesque bulk, from this monstrous, metallic skeleton towering to the ceiling with its great maw in front ready to grab you, to digest you. You ran back up the stairs.

After lunch, Ed lay down on the sofa to listen to the game. Trish came home and helped you fill the bathtub with torn paper and dollops of glue. Forbidden to go into the depths, she pouted for a while until you gave permission to go to the birthday party. You carried the sodden mess to the basement in a pail and began to pelt the thing without focusing on it. Ed appeared once then retreated when he saw the look on your ink-stained face. Up and down two flights you flew in a frenzy of loathing, stopping only to lob the wet paper, slipping on the floor, now and then emitting a manic snarl. It didn't take long; something disgusting in you even wanted to go on, but this morning's *Journal* did the trick, capped the peak, added its dripping weight to the groaning plywood. Without looking back, you slammed the basement door. Even with the game on, the constant splash of a thousand drops of water echoed through the house. Thank God Ed had cleaned the floor drain this summer.

The thing dripped all night, the sound magnified in the heating vents. It took two Rosaries before you fell into a troubled sleep to dream of subterranean caverns and their vile denizens. Before Mass, Ed went down to feel it; he came back encouraged.

"Just a little damp. You can start painting after dinner."

"Honey, I can't go down there again."

"Well, do I have to paint it too? Whose project is this anyway? Why can't our darling daughter do it?"

"I don't want her down there either. I said she could go to the show."

Dinner was very quiet, the only semblance of a conversation occurring when you wondered about calling the Monsignor for a dispensation for Sunday work and were told curtly that if this wasn't an emergency, what was? and don't be so scrupulous. Ed gulped the rest of his food, changed clothes, and went down. At two, he emerged with third-degree smears. He must have fallen into it. Or did it . . . ?

"I didn't have enough gray. Had to finish with brown. Wally's coming around four."

Ed's brother backed his pickup across the lawn to the outside cellar doors. He would take the thing to his warehouse overnight to dry. Ed would join him in the morning to help deliver it before first period. Wally was a furniture mover, an expert. It would be a piece of cake.

Ed didn't close the basement door. Some dark premonition told you to leave it open too, so you sipped black coffee at the kitchen table and heard it all. Wally said don't even bother to pick it up, it wouldn't go. Ed said the cellar doors were double. Remember the skiff he built? It fit. Wally said this wasn't a skiff, it was the Queen Mary. They grunted and hollered and worse for nearly an hour. Then there was a long, eerie silence. When the cellar doors slammed shut, you jumped, spilling your cup. As the pickup ground another set of furrows into the lawn, Ed came up to ask for a piece of clean paper and the name of that Sister.

Trish sniffled through breakfast as if bent on again unleashing the torrent upon which she had sailed disconsolately since her return from the movies the evening before. Her tear ducts, however, apparently had been exhausted. All she could manage was an ungracious whine as she shoved the envelope into her religion book. You went upstairs to look at Our Lady in the bedroom, the Immaculate Heart. She pointed to the flame of love in her breast. You asked for compassion, mercy, a miracle, anything she could do. She smiled. It had been your mother's picture. You liked to remember your mother smiling like that. You prayed a mother's prayer, the first of many that day.

"Hi."

It wasn't like Trish to come home later than her father. When she finally banged through the door at five-thirty, you both drew a breath of relief. She made her usual beeline for the refrigerator.

"Well?"

"Um. We had volleyball for P.E. and decided to play for awhile after."

"What about the thing, the project?"

"Um. Oh, Sister said since so many weren't ready, she'd give us all another week."

As you went upstairs to see the lady with the heart, Ed was calling Wally. Something about borrowing his chain saw.

❖

"And from that hour the disciple took her into his house." There we keep her still, a symbol of all that is right with the world, the lady who came to stay. For two thousand years, poets have sung her praises, theologians have delineated her virtues, churchmen and women have polished her pedestal: holy, chaste, obedient, humble, faithful, first of the redeemed. To most of us, however, unversed as we are in ecclesiastical rhetoric, she is simply the Good Mother. Like the best of mothers, Mary is always there, always listening, interested in our smallest concerns, ready to intercede on behalf of our best intentions.

There are some who say that she gets in the way, that praying to the Mother of Christ or to any of our brothers and sisters in the communion of saints somehow subverts the cool logic of "to the Father through the Son in the Holy Spirit". In the realm of bloodless theory, this argument has a certain allure. Why clutter up your relationship to the Trinity, why seek other mediators when the Son of God was anointed for this ministry and gave his life to prove its efficacy? But there is another kind of logic that flourishes in the faults and fissures of life. It is the unlearned, almost automatic attraction to the familiar in time of need. When you were chastised unfairly by your English teacher, you didn't run to the principal; he was unworldly, strange, perhaps not even of your species. You ran to your mother because her love was tangible, instantly available, and above all, familiar. Of course, this was a failure in what theoreticians call logic. You should have gone to that great, echoing office, stated your case in piping words of one syllable, and received swift justice. That's the way the system was supposed to work. The wise child, though, knew that the system sometimes broke down and even when functioning properly demanded a flight into the unknown. Even if your mother was powerless to make the matter right, her ways were comprehensible and, most important, she was there, present with her consolation.

Consolation is the key to the appeal of the Blessed Virgin. Yes, we seek her intercession in the fulfillment of our desires, but when the operation of the divine will is contrary to that hoped for, we are not bereft, for a mother's love is independent of the success of her children's petitions. When your mother took your plea to the principal and was denied for reasons known only to godlike authority, she did not love you less, she loved you more in your disappointment. The Mother of Christ, who had seen so many of her hopes for her son dashed in Nazareth, in Jerusalem, and on Calvary, knows the necessity of solace and favors the brokenhearted with her understanding presence.

It is an irony that, in spite of the renewed communitarian emphasis in most Western churches, so many believers pay little heed to the doctrine of the communion of saints. So successfully has secular society championed self-sufficiency that to rely on anyone else, even God, seems an invitation to humiliation. Those who give a grudging nod in the direction of the Almighty as having at least a bit of an edge, choke on a prayer to a fellow human being no matter what state of glory he may have achieved. This refusal to seek the intercession of a resident of heaven guarantees less than effective prayer. Just as the contemporary breakdown of family life strangles in coils of loneliness the obtusely individualistic, so the narrow, go-it-alone spiritual life squeezes out the assistance offered by heavenly patrons and stifles the camaraderie of common goals sought by the faithful and realized by the saints. There is so much familial warmth hanging over this chilly world and so few willing to admit their need of it. Mary, the lady with the heart, is the epitome of this waiting grace, grace unfortunately gone a'wasting.

Turn to her, good Christian, and to her children gone before us. She is our Good Mother; they, our victorious brothers and sisters. Your woes are no match for her trials; your hopes, their attained glory. Prayers to the saints and to their Queen do not demean you any more than your recourse to your elders when you were a child. On God's green earth, we are still little ones struggling toward fulfillment. Especially in times of difficulty, there await intercessors who call out in the logic of faults and fissures. And one, above all, who prayed to Yahweh for her son's consolation, waits to ask for solace and light in your confusion. They are family, offering solidarity to self-orphaned sisters and brothers. She is Mother, tender in her attention, constant in her concern, the lady with the heart.

In the fissures deep between
rampant famines, warring nations,
lie my little woes unseen,
undistinguished tribulations.

Feather-light on heaven's scale
is this leaden apprehension,
nonetheless in dread I quail,
begging gentle condescension.

Who will note this puny cry
prompted by a childish nightmare,
in a cosmos gone awry
is there anyone who might care?

Enters she who always heeds
anguish in the smallest matters,
with a silver chain of beads
binding up a world in tatters.

Hail, Good Mother, holy one,
never done with interceding;
comfort of your blessed Son,
bend to this poor pilgrim's pleading.
   Amen.

Sounds in Silence

A strong and heavy wind was rending the mountain
and crushing rocks before the Lord—but the Lord
was not in the wind. After the wind there was an
earthquake—but the Lord was not in the earthquake.
After the earthquake there was fire—but the Lord was
not in the fire. After the fire there was a tiny whispering sound. When he heard this, Elijah hid his face in
his cloak and went and stood at the entrance of the
cave. A voice said to him, "Elijah, why are you here?"
(1 Kings 19:11–13).

It was as if the world had suddenly stopped turning, as if
the power-driven rush of schedule and deadline had been
frozen for an instant, the whole flesh and metal machinery of enterprise held in check to give you time to ease
around projecting demands, slip from paralyzed palms.
Present and absent, they all stood there—co-workers, children, friends, typewriters, taxis, vacuum cleaners—silent
as you made your way through them to the telephone. Unable to raise a protesting hand or grind a gear of warning,
they heard your query, your request, your thanks, noting
with skepticism the resolution in your voice. You wouldn't,
you couldn't do this to them.

That was Tuesday, not at all a good-news day. You had
to take a break, make a break before you broke. Now, fifty
miles from the city, increasingly suspicious of your rash
action, you hurriedly unpack a thin suitcase. It seems important to get your things into the tiny closet, to pull on

143

sneakers, important to belong here and nowhere else this Friday áfternoon. Some sort of anchor is needed, some quickly spreading root system to oppose the tug of common sense already making the maelstrom you left seem almost benign. Even as you escaped the last crowded street, the power of the familiar urged you into U-turn lanes. With every mile, heedless determination gave way to inexorable logic. What was wrong with working it out at home? A few minutes with the Lord in a closed room had seen you through many trials. Why trek to this deserted spot, why make such a production of it? Wasn't God everywhere? You thought of all the life you would be missing this weekend. How lovely are your traffic jams, O Lord, my God. And all those ambivalent farewells as you left, masked accusations of overblown piety. Have a good one, they said. Holier-than-thou, they meant.

"Silence begins at six with supper", sibilance from a brown cowl as sandaled feet padded down the soundless hall before you. Brother Matthew had been a bit off the mark. Silence as another thing, as a palpable presence, really began when you switched off the radio and stepped onto the gravel drive. It was not the absence of other sounds that magnified the scrunch of your feet on the stones; wind soughed in the trees, birds chirped. Rather, it was something under this canopy of leaves that demanded of the most discreet movement a password. There was a force in this forest obliging the thump of a trunk lid or the jingle of keys as audible warnings that an intruder was loose in Elysium. You quickly stepped off the path, making your way to the oaken door on neatly clipped, unprotesting grass. Matthew was waiting, obviating the need for strident buzzer or thunderous knock. Above his head, carved deeply into the weathered lintel, was the name of the beast: *Silentium*.

144

The bed emits a harsh squawk as you sit on it, making you feel guilty again, reminding you of Matthew's bony finger at his lips as you thanked him too loudly in the hall. You can't back out now, at least not tonight. Tomorrow, some mumbled excuse will do, stomach flu, perhaps, and then a long drive upstate to that little fishing village of happy memory, arriving after dark in the midst of raucous voices telling of the ones that got away. Not easy to get a room this time of year. Well, you hadn't stayed up all night in the lounge of a motel since college. It would prove your mettle. A nap in the car, maybe rent some tackle, find a clear, swift stream, then back to town on Sunday night, exhausted from your spiritual ordeal, too tired to talk about it except to say how much you needed it.

Five forty-five. A gong, and two more. Approved, of course. Holy sounds. Reason understood. In the halls a few handshakes. Others looking silly with pursed lips, kids on Halloween sneaking up to someone's garden statuary. In the refectory a bald brother with a beavertail beard sits on a dais in the corner reading the rule the Founder set down a thousand years ago, competing with the mad clicking of salt and pepper shakers passed endlessly among surprised guests striving to make something more of the thin soup. You look around quickly as your jaw pops in the effort to accommodate the thick slices of dark bread and pale cheese. Could anyone hear what you are doing to this driest of all sandwiches? The reading stops before the apples are finished. Snap and crunch shiver the air. Matthew rises to introduce the directors. You are in the first flight: 7:00 p.m., room 2. He suggests a visit to the chapel first. You go to your room and begin packing.

Father Basil says nothing. Despite his kindly eyes, now politely focused on the middle distance, you get the feeling of disapproval. Has he some intuition that your bag is back in the car? You had told your story well enough, bringing to life in this bare room your *bête noire*, that premonition of doom born of unmet quotas, unmanageable children, uncomprehending spouse. The burden had been bearable for some months until the day you lost contact with the Lord. You endured for another two weeks; then last Tuesday, you stopped the world and got off. Silence. You spoke with feeling of self-pity and lack of direction, inviting with your earnestness even the most oblique response. Suddenly recalling that this was not the first of five scheduled conferences but the only one, you let your voice trail off; no use making this kind of investment. Silence. You listen to your breathing, to his, to the cry of a water bird on the wing. Going north? Going fishing?

"Yes, it is quiet." Your hand jumps on the arm of the chair. "Here we get used to it, but our guests from the city find it very difficult. Listening, weren't you? For my wise comments, I suppose, then for anything. A lady from Chicago once told me she could hear the El. Please understand that I'm not supposed to say much, maybe nothing at all. As to your questions about whether you were doing right in your home situation or in that sticky business with the boss, that's not my department. I'm here to help you listen, not to solve your problems. That's why the first night is the toughest. People want to lay things out, to set an agenda. This dilemma tomorrow morning, that one in the afternoon. It doesn't work that way here." From the front of the building comes the whir of a starter. Your hand jumps again. Then careful tires on tattletale stones. "It sounds like Father Gregory just lost a customer. My main job tonight is to keep you from following that car."

"I've already got my bag in the trunk. I was going to wait 'til tomorrow, but the silence at supper got to me. Can you give me one good reason to stay?"

146

"Only that you're here and not there. It wasn't good there. If you go back now, nothing will have changed. By coming here you proved something, that you wanted things to change. They have already. Whether for good or ill remains to be seen, or should I say, heard, but you'll never know if you leave now."

"But isn't there some kind of exercise, some prayer? Note taking. How about note taking? I did that once a couple of years ago. It seemed to help for a while."

"No, nothing like that. Just listening."

"For what? Tell me what to listen for."

"For nothing. Certainly not for answers, not even for the Lord. Just listen. Go to the chapel and listen. If you hear the creak of a kneeler or someone's stomach, it is enough. In bed tonight, listen to the house settle, listen to the plumbing knock. In the morning, take a walk to the lake. Listen to the waves. Then come back at nine and tell me what you heard."

"But I didn't have to come all this way to do that. I could listen at home."

"Pardon me, my friend, but with all due respect, obviously you couldn't. You heard a lot of noise, all right, but not *your* sounds."

"You mean the sounds I make?"

"No, I mean the sounds made for you, those which are yours and yours alone." He holds up his hand. "That's enough for tonight. I hear my next victim in the hall."

His chuckle follows you out, a welcome bit of self-mockery, easing the suspicion of being patronized. A nice guy, but one of those Eastern Rite dreamers you had been warned about, locked away from the real world for too long. Your pastor had told you that all these monks thought they belonged on Mount Athos.

On the way to your room to see if you left anything, you

147

pass the chapel. A kneeler creaks. The lone supplicant gen-
uflects, then leaves by a side door. A little prayer wouldn't
hurt. Saint Christopher for a safe trip in the dark. Saint
Peter for good fishing. In the pew, the chuckle comes back,
and the loon's cry, and the tires on the driveway. A branch
scrapes the roof in the soft wind. Your sound. There is no
one else to hear it. A sound for you alone. What does it
mean? Nothing, he said, just a sound. But yours.

No sense in driving all night. Bright and early tomorrow
get a fresh start with breakfast. Maybe they'll serve real
food. Maybe see him again at nine. Hear him one last time.
Will he chuckle? That would be enough.

❖

Although in a noisy world a lot of praying must be done
in the midst of distracting voices, not every distraction can
be lumped under the heading of noise. The baby's cry that
takes you from your Bible at 11:00 p.m. is not noise. The
doorbell that violates your prayer nook on a quiet Saturday afternoon is not noise if it announces a friend having
a difficult time in her bereavement. There are all kinds of
buzzers and gongs, announcements and pleas to which we
should respond if the kingdom of God is to be furthered. A
time comes, however, when proportion must be restored to
the life of the spirit; indeed, so necessary is a periodic reap-
praisal of our reactions to the demands made upon us, so
inhospitable to extended meditation is the hurly-burly of
the everyday, that escape is the only recourse.

In a society that places such a high value on ambition
and self-sufficiency, the word "escape" has a pejorative ring
to it. One who needs to escape is seen as weak, as some-

how lacking the gumption to prevail in business, parenting, or even in the spiritual endeavor. Those who do step back from the contest are expected to come up with an acceptable euphemism for their obvious faintheartedness. I am going on a nature walk. You are taking a study week. She is recharging her batteries. He is analyzing his options. None of us is escaping, for that would mean things got out of hand, events overwhelmed us. We are not fleeing, we are advancing in a different direction.

The wise Christian knows that there is no dishonor in the kind of escape offered by a spiritual retreat. The world does have the power to drown out the essential word, to desensitize the most receptive soul. Those who boast of the ability to respond to every demand often let expedience have the final say, but when there is no time to rest in the Lord, the chances of hearing his loving affirmation are slim. True, he is always there calling out in the distress of stricken brothers and sisters, but he is also in Elijah's gentle breeze. From time to time, that tiny whispering sound must be pursued in a place apart.

A cautionary note is appropriate here. Certain aspects of the retreat movement speak in accents disturbingly similar to the language of progress. Enneagrams, journaling, various regimens and exercises based on personality inventories promise, or at least encourage the pursuit of, successful reintegration of the psycho-spiritual construct. While these may or may not be valid claims, such progress should be secondary to the need of the din-dazed pilgrim for the simple serenity of silence. Saint John of the Cross wrote: "The Father uttered one Word; that Word is his Son, and he utters him for ever in everlasting silence; and in silence the world has to hear it." Despite the psychological benefits that may result from the various forms of the "power retreat", many people in this clamorous age would be better served in learning the sounds of silence, for one of them is the Sound uttered by the Father.

The greatest obstacle to the choice of a retreat based on silence is fear. Even those who treasure their twenty-minute tastes of heaven in a place only partially protected from the clatter of home life are intimidated by the thought of three days of absolute quiet. Common sense protests. We need the company of others as sounding boards, as recipients of our voiced thoughts; their counterpoint provides direction and moderation for our ideas. Alone, without a balancing opinion, we might fly out of orbit, become silly or depressed, lose touch with reality. This fear of protracted silence in solitude is essentially a fear of self and a lack of trust in God, part of the rattling continuum of doubt that led us to consider such a retreat in the first place. Thus, the original decision to open ourselves to the unknown, to go to a place apart and unpopulated, is by far the most important and difficult step in the process. On our return, we may be hard put to articulate the insights gained, but time and memory will assure us that our faith in God and self was never stronger than it was at the moment when we lifted the receiver and made the reservation. Whoever was at the other end of the line heard a few dry facts—date of arrival, length of stay—but the Father heard an avowal of trust, a plea from a noisy world for healing silence, and a word of willingness to listen for a Word of wisdom.

Wait not too long to seek the silence. There is a place apart not far away, a retreat house or a monastery, where learned directors lead the distracted to contemplate tiny sounds. They know better than you how daunting days and nights of silence can be; they know too the joy in simple listening, the solace in hearing the message of God's love in the cry of a bird, in the soft stirring of an evening breeze, in the branch rubbing the window inviting a nervous guest to gaze upon a grove of ancient oaks. In giving yourself to these gentle guides and their quiet routine, you have nothing to fear and much to hope for. In listening, your shriveled soul will expand with new-found sensitivity to God's whisperings, your heart will be filled with the sounds of a new creation, a world made just for you. You will come to know the soothing balm of holy silence, and that the hardest part was over when you put down the telephone. There is a place for you nearby, a place alive with sounds the Father offers you alone, and, yes, the Word he utters through eternity. Wait not too long.

❖

birds a'chirp remembering
Eden's first light
wind in willows heralding
love's rout of night
drip of dew encouraging
dark into day
teach the morning lesson, Lord,
your quiet way

shrill cicadas shattering
noon's lazy dream
panting spaniel challenging
trout in the stream
muffled thunder echoing
heaven's hushed sway
share this midday wisdom, Lord,
your peaceful way

whir of nightwings pivoting
under the eaves
soft applause uncovering
pale-bosomed leaves
lowing cattle lumbering
home from the hay
give me evening solace, Lord,
your restful way
                Amen.

Harvest

John answered them all, saying, "I am baptizing you
with water, but one mightier than I is coming. I am
not worthy to loosen the thongs of his sandals. He
will baptize you with the holy Spirit and fire. His win-
nowing fan is in his hand to clear his threshing floor
and to gather the wheat into his barn, but the chaff he
will burn with unquenchable fire." Exhorting them
in many other ways, he preached good news to the
people (Luke 3:16–18).

So heavy was the grain upon the slender stalks that it hung
upside down, presenting to the benign sky a million tawny
arches, a birthing blanket of acres and sections woven in
hope. From the north end of the great field, a zephyr would
dip and dance, bidding the wheat to rise, to look upon
a shared luxuriance, a common effort come to fruit. The
playful wind would scamper rapidly up and down and then
away, for it would do no good to let these bearded heads
stand straight for long or turn with a dallying breeze to
the south, to peer over a golden roll of earth and gape at
puffs of two-cycle smoke inching closer. It was enough for
these ears to hear and bend again in docile optimism to the
unknown growlcrankratchet of pulleys and gears and os-
cillating scythes.

Soon enough would come the Arbiter, a bulbous green
machine combining flashing knives and tumbling beds to
slice and vibrate, strip and blow. The chaff would settle like

soulful snow upon the stubble, the treasure would cascade into the back of a groaning truck in overflowing abundance. What matter a little spill, for the field was endless; each knoll revealed another vista of bounty, or to the sweating men, another hour of sun-blanched toil.

They ate at one o'clock, struck down between life and death, lying in the strict shade under the rear of the combine. From the tailgate of her pickup, wife and mother funneled slabs of ham, haphazardly mashed potatoes, gallons of ice-cold milk into her men. She hurried to fill them, for this was but a faint promise of what was bubbling on her stoves and baking in her ovens until full dark. Then they would sit down around the oilcloth and eat. Now they merely swallowed, gulped seven hours of strength, pumped stomachs against belts to see if they were full. They always wanted more; even as the plume of dust behind her little truck disappeared, they wanted more, wanted it to be eight o'clock.

At four, a gusty thunderhead appeared to mixed petitions. The hired man wished it would open wide with a deluge like that which topped Ararat, a statement from God himself that this day had gone on long enough. He took his hand from the wheel and touched the bare metal of the grain truck's roof making the sweat on his callused finger sizzle. The farmer stood up from the tractor seat imploring the Almighty to push the dark specter away. He wanted no gift from the sky until the last acre was down. The boys were ambivalent. Glistening roads . . . Saturday night in town . . . the stamp of feet at the Stardust. God knows they deserved it after three straight weeks in the dust. They kept shoveling, though, remembering last September's week of rain when they scraped and repainted the stalls in the hog house.

This wind did not caper. A moist palm slapped the rest

of the field, straining for a brief eternity the slim arches remaining, then let up suddenly, allowing heads bent low all day to spring skyward and behold the serried devastation. Once more the sharp rain flattened them, then again, and then it was over, leaving each stalk mantled in sparkling beads, standing tall in the aftergusts until earth recalled abundance to itself.

The boys leaned on their shovels, the hired man thrummed the gear shift as the farmer walked among his now-alarmed creation. Wisps of wheat clung to his legs, pulled at his boots, vain restraint against the judgment. He lifted his head where they could not and hollered back. "Not too bad!" In the truck, the dashboard received a vicious blow and clanging shovels muffled a puerile curse.

They would finish the field today, even at half speed through the wet grain. The tattered cloud absorbed the sun's strongest rays; the rain had laid the dust. The roof of the cab was almost cool. The boys, however, were on double time, tossing the grain high to dry it, moving it from back to front in the giant box, mixing it with the crisp kernels at the bottom. The breeze at their backs, their exhaustion, and their father's inattention at this slow pace made them silly. They wrestled in the cool drifts, jousted with their shovels, spit the precious harvest at each other. Abruptly aware that the procession had stopped once more, they raised their eyes to see the old man glaring at them, then turned to follow his finger along the trail of treasure they had kicked over the side. The eldest climbed down warily as his father came back to the truck with a gunny sack. "All of it and no dirt." Stooping for the first handful, he glanced at those bowed legs marching again to the tractor, and beyond, at the last two acres of crop black against the setting sun.

There was some forced conversation around the table:

heavy wheat and four days of fan drying and whether the belting would take it. She reported that the Hufts had quit early because of the rain. He said Ozzie Huft would quit early if he got sweat in his eye and that was why it always snowed on their last half section. The boys said now that only one field was left they should get a day off, and he said maybe they should hire out over at the Hufts if they wanted to play games. The hired man said nothing, thinking as usual of Wichita's exotic night life. It was the same as every supper during the harvest, just a few monosyllables to keep from choking. What strength they had left was for eating, not for talking.

By nine-thirty they were all locked in dreamless sleep. Beyond the creek, over in the last field of standing grain, powdery chaff blew softly a whispered lament among slender stalks.

None of us, no matter how firm our belief in the resurrection, can afford to camouflage or depreciate what must come first: the harvest. Nine First Fridays or nine hundred will not make of the final crisis a walk in the woods. Whether after months of suffering in a cancer ward or with the searing flash of an electrical shock, there will come the most painful of life's perceptions, that of our powerlessness in the definitive struggle. The acknowledgment of one's inability to protect and prolong a once self-animating, self-extensive, self-sufficient existence marks the end of that existence. After that agonizing admission, life is radically changed. Nor can it return to what it was. Unlike exhaustion or despair or sinfulness, this new state is irreversible. The body senses finality, strains vainly to muster meager resources; the spirit, even in light of the Easter promise, shrinks back, shamelessly inconstant, undone by a view of the abyss. Death is knowing, believing, appreciating that we are incapable of the alternative. We teeter on the edge of darkness, wondering what happened to all our prayers for a happy death.

Yet, in the midst of this paralysis, there will remain active the most human of all faculties, the ability to choose. The habit of prayer for a happy death must be based on an understanding of the ultimate decision, must include an awareness of the tenacity of the life force and the horror of the unknown, an awareness sharpened by a daily petition for the strength that eventually will be needed to overcome these restraints in favor of doing God's will. Today, under blue skies and sunny prospects, it is easy to embrace his pledge of a glorified existence on the other side, but how strong will be our grip as the precipice rises from the mist? Even one more moment in this vale of tears will seem preferable to the leap of faith demanded at the last instant. It is clear that the committed Christian's habit of choosing the way of the Lord must not weaken as death approaches. Our prayer then is that we might remain human, that we might continue to decide rightly until the end.

Prayer for a happy death should not be a plea that we be carried willy-nilly into eternity, but that we will make our last choice correctly, that it will be a part of the continuum of decisions we have made all our lives. Thus, seemingly inconsequential choices take on a new importance, and the others, those that cost us so dearly, changing our lives on the spot, traumatizing our souls for weeks and months afterward, are seen as paradigmatic. It would be naïve to think that the supreme exercise of our free will could be any less agonizing. So while it is salutary to pray for a happy death, we recognize that joy will be evident not so much in the act as in the subsequent confirmation of the

157

rightness of a wrenching choice. Gritted teeth, wavering faith, sorrow over the loss of the familiar, all the unavoidable circumstances surrounding the last breath are not the stuff of joy. We pray instead for the happy outcome of our most difficult decision.

Like the golden grain in the fields, most of us are surprised by death. We toss our heads and tell ourselves that those puffs of smoke on the horizon are going in another direction. Unlike the wheat, however, we can determine whether we shall be gathered into the bins or blown away with the chaff. The moment of truth will be one more operation of the will supported or undermined by all the choices that have gone before it. Therefore, the most authentic, most effective prayer for a happy death is the daily petition that we might choose rightly in the few hours between now and tomorrow. Into this short space of time will come one or two challenges to test our faithfulness to God's plan. In magnitude they will pale in comparison to the final test, but in essence each will be a rehearsal for that last leap. Pray that each will be a leap of faith.

❖

so unforeseen the final flight
last fluttering of life from brittle limb
once gleaming wings now grizzled
stiffly stretching to catch a rising breath
against the waxing heave of gravity

gnarled talons loosen in the fickle wind
dream and hope fly skyward
as earth fills a yellowed eye
snapping in surprise
at the rocks uprushing

plummets the master of the air
in such undignified descent
cartwheeling to stony rest
a clash of fragile skeleton and shale
heard only in high heaven

bear me up, Lord, on that day
when age outweighs this raven soul
release me as an eagle
ascending ever from the splash
of blood and feathers on the nettled crag
Amen.

I Had a Dream

Jesus raised his eyes to heaven and said:
"I pray not only for them,
but also for those who will believe in me
    through their word,
so that they may all be one,
as you, Father, are in me and I in you,
that they also may be in us,
that the world may believe that you sent me.
And I have given them the glory you gave me,
so that they may be one, as we are one,
I in them and you in me,
that they may be brought to perfection as one,
that the world may know that you sent me,
and that you loved them even as you loved me."

(John 17:20–23)

The heat seemed to go out of the August sun as the march knifed into Pollman Park. You weren't shivering, of course; even fear couldn't make teeth chatter when the temperature stood just below the century mark. The chill was interior, coiling around your heart, hobbling its beat to match the steady shuffle of a thousand feet. High summer, hot time in the city, open hydrants and cool theaters; instead, you found yourself parboiled on the outside and freeze-dried on the inside after two hours of hurry-up-and-wait on the oozing asphalt. Downtown, it hadn't been so bad. The Sunday skyscrapers cast vacant shadows in the canyons. You could even sit on the cool sidewalk and lis-

ten to last-minute instructions bouncing off the buildings.
The march captain seemed to have no head, just a bullhorn
mounted on ebony shoulders:

"Do not answer. No matter what they say, no matter
what you think you hear, no backtalk. Keep singing.
Even if you can't hear anybody else, keep singing.
Even if you can't sing, keep singing. Keep your eyes
open for rocks and bottles. Catch them if you can,
but drop them. Don't throw them back. We are not at
war with anybody. We are fighting attitudes. Let them
show their attitudes to the press. Don't lag. Don't fall
out. Don't leave the line. Watch your marshal. Get his
number and keep your eye on him until we come out
the other side. WATCH YOUR MARSHAL!"

You wondered about coming out the other side as your
row passed the Realty Board's sign of welcome to this
all-white enclave. "City of Progress", it read. "Home of
Pollman Pirates: State Senior Baseball Champions. Exclu-
sive Homesites Available." There would be some pitch-
ers warming up today. The frost had begun to form on
your heart when the marshals lost their bearings some six
blocks back. Letting the Metro Police guide you with their
noncommittal eyes, they had all moved to the front of the
column to get a better view of the attitudes that waited
on either side of what would become Main Street. When
they came back to the ranks, few could find their stations.
They huddled, stopped the march twice just on the city
line, then haphazardly reassigned themselves. There was
tension among them, that same cold hand of fear that con-
stricted your heart, white knuckles clutching the wheel
when the brakes fail. Were these the attitudes you and the
other foot soldiers were sent out to exploit?

It was impossible to see around the big black woman

who marched in front of you. "Eyes front, eyes front!" screamed the jumpy marshals, so you simply followed her ubiquitous flesh and listened as the citizens welcomed the three hundred who preceded you. The curses were sporadic and not very inventive. You answered with your mouth closed. Even your silent replies were mild and understanding, befitting the high calling of the martyr.

The regular undulations of the big woman's body, the milling marshals' frightened pleas for custody of the eyes, the monotonous repetition of the catcalls all combined to lull you into a stupor. You didn't spot the boy with the bucket until he ran up to challenge the woman in front. Over her shoulder you saw his grotesque face, flesh pulled back like the man on the 2000-mph sled. No words, just a screech. Then he took a breath and threw the red paint at her. Blinded, she went down in a heap, allowing you to see how the boy had gotten so close. There was no one else there; the ranks in front of her had disintegrated. Hundreds of marchers were scattering in panic, tripping over fallen comrades as a torrent of bottles and bricks poured from the roofs of the low buildings. Behind you too, the march came apart; you could hear feet running back to the city line, back to where the police protection had stopped. Your companions called to you as they raced for the blue lights stroking the welcome sign. The woman was struggling with her voluminous skirt, using it to swab her eyes. You stripped off your T-shirt and gave it to her. As her sight returned, she cried softly to see your white skin; she cried for the target you had made of yourself out there in the middle of that boiling black river. You remembered just in time the demonstration given by the march captain, the one about the most effective way of protecting yourself in a clubbing. The bat filled your vision; just two blows, two home runs for the state championship team, and the slugger moved to another diamond. You and the woman stumbled back to the police cars. You leaned on her to save your shattered kneecap; sightless again, she maneuvered according to your shouted directions. Her name turned out to be Marvella.

❖

The heady atmosphere of brotherhood that fueled those civil rights marches has all but disappeared today. It is a mistake to say that the sweet sense of dangers shared and common yearnings gave way to reality. Among many blacks and whites then, solidarity *was* reality. Bull Connor and his ilk were real, and they saw to it that people were really beaten. The counterforce of love linking the marchers was real, substantial, tactile. A colorblind society was as real as Christ in the Eucharist, hidden from the eye of the cynic but a dream come to life for the believer. The dream never gave way to reality. Reality itself changed and the dream, cut loose from relevance, drifted away and died for lack of attention.

So happily surprised were they over our pledges of unity that the people of the underclass were disposed to overlook our naïve patronizing. "We shall overcome", sang we who had nothing to overcome. They sang it with us for a while, but soon chose a different register, an alien beat, the African rhythms of independence. We didn't learn quickly enough that freedom was but a step toward self-determination. Our soft-edged espousals of universal dignity began to sound rather silly against a background of cities crackling with flames and the strident voices of black militancy. Tired of defending the hyperbole of pressure groups and urban terrorists, many of us fled the arena to nurse our bruised liberalism. Reality had changed, the plates of the substrata had shifted; it was us and them again separated by a crack in the earth. We changed our tune to a solo: "Let it be."

Prejudice is again socially acceptable because so many idealists thought it could be conquered for good. In dignifying an idealized version of our domestic exiles while ignoring their absolute need for power, the liberal salved his conscience at the expense of the new reality. Now, after the earthquake of black power, the pain of disappointment is too great, the cost of rapprochement too high to resume the quest for unity. It is easier to dream of what might have been, easier to curse the pesky human needs that fouled the machinery of brotherhood than to humble ourselves to learn Jesus' way of bridging the chasm. In his final discourse, he prayed "that they may all be one". But words were not enough. His way required that prayer take flesh; the next day he would die to manifest his solidarity with all humankind. Twenty-five years ago, you put your life on the line for an ideal, your dream of happiness for a whole people. As things turned out, it wasn't their dream for themselves. Now, you must practice the fine and humbling art of listening. Let them tell you how the picture you painted differs from their self-portrait. Before unity must come equality. Before equality must come reality. Before reality must come humility.

When the reality of a people's demand for dignity becomes especially urgent and strident voices make scathing, all-inclusive charges of prejudice, even the most fair-minded Christian may feel therapeutic humility turn to humiliation and then to resentment. The shock of this illiberal reaction triggers a flight to prayer as an island of serenity in a world deaf to good intentions. In the stillness of meditation, we ask the gracious Savior to soothe our misunderstood souls with his healing touch. All of us know that prayer. All of us need it. Yet, some of us will admit that it is not enough to nestle in the Lord's lap and ask him to call down a miracle of amity. The remedy for conflict among groups is the kind of mutual openness that only one individual can offer another.

To be sure, prayer must precede any attempt to rebuild trust, but we must be prudent in our objectives. There is nothing wrong in asking God to open the heart of another, to make him more understanding, to lead him to tolerance. Such petitions, however, fall into the category of fond hopes unless the primary focus of the prayer for brotherhood centers on our own attitudes. The battleground is my heart. To wish to linger undisturbed in the affirming presence of the Lord is natural and quite necessary to the refreshment of our lagging spirits, but the Holy Spirit will soon announce the truth: To call forth change in others, we must change first.

Contemporary prayer, no matter how classic the form, is subject to contemporary pressures. As the struggle for dignity among classes, races, and sexes interrupts our contemplative repose, and the cry of the marginalized awakens us from self-satisfied dreams of impartiality, the dynamic Spirit of unity attacks the barriers we have thrown up around ourselves. We are led to a holy impatience with our smugness, and we are in good company, for the persistent reality of discrimination exhausts even the patience of Christ. He stands up from his throne, depriving us of the lap in which we sought solace, forcing us to reshape our own approach to those beyond the pale. It is a rude awakening that even the most conciliatory Christian must acknowledge.

While prayer for mutual respect on a universal scale may be valid, it is certainly quite thin. Good intentions this nebulous are not enough by half. Authentic prayer always produces a change in the one who prays. In the matter of prejudice, this change can be painful, but Christ's vision of human harmony demands that each of us first look inward. There, at the center where all pretense is swept away, begins the concord for which Jesus prayed. "That they may be one, as we are one, I in them and you in me, that they may be brought to perfection as one."

❖

The pulse of life
beneath the skin,
the flow of hope
that makes us kin,
the striving hearts
which beat as one,
the blood we share
with God's own Son
belie the cant
proclaiming fate
has destined us
to hurt and hate.
O Lord, must you
once more pour out
that crimson stream
upon our doubt
to wash away
disunity
and prove by death
our dignity?
    Amen.

Ruby Begonia

Put on then, as God's chosen ones, holy and beloved,
heartfelt compassion, kindness, humility, gentleness,
and patience, bearing with one another and forgiving
one another, if one has a grievance against another; as
the Lord has forgiven you, so must you also do. And
over all these put on love, that is, the bond of perfection. And let the peace of Christ control your hearts,
the peace into which you were also called in one body.
And be thankful. Let the word of Christ dwell in you
richly, as in all wisdom you teach and admonish one
another, singing psalms, hymns, and spiritual songs
with gratitude in your hearts to God. And whatever
you do, in word or in deed, do everything in the name
of the Lord Jesus, giving thanks to God the Father
through him. (Colossians 3:12–17)

Only the foolhardy would dare call it "the back yard". It
was her kingdom, always had been. She wouldn't even allow you to mow what little space she had allotted to grass.
Yours were the garage and its environs, the driveway, the
front lawn with its dandelions; in her magnanimity she had
even given you charge of the flower boxes on the porch
railing. You put in geraniums, six on each side, all red, and
red petunias along the sidewalk. You did your best. You
watered them from May through October, not with any
set schedule, but enough to make them bloom. You pulled

the crabgrass from the lawn and edged the driveway and washed the mildew off the garage. More often than most husbands, you had grass stains on your overalls and potting soil under your fingernails. For your irregular labors you had an incentive, though it always remained unspoken.

It was up to you to provide the comparison for the visitors who took the short walk that led to another dimension. The gate between the garage and the back corner of the house would click; voices would rise as the difference between your world and hers became apparent. Your world was like theirs with its share of weeds and drooping petals. Her world was alternating concentric circles of asters and marigolds, flagstone walks bordered in daffodils and daylilies, a world bounded by trellises thick with yellow, gold, and white roses. Around the glistening oak was a collar of mixed orange and violet impatiens. Circling the two white birches were dahlias and bleeding hearts, delicate pink against the slim white trunks. Did the guests hear falling water? Step through an arch woven of jasmine and wisteria to marvel at a marble fountain from the Appian Way. Tired? Let the zinnias lead you to a noble stone bench said to have given respite to Aristotle's logical bones.

The reaction of the visitors had become predictable. First, delight—the hypnotic joy spurred by the delicate blending and contrast of fuchsia, cherry, burgundy, violet, lavender, gentian, magenta, peach, and salmon. One home and garden columnist had described it as Oz come to life; another as almost an out-of-body experience. Then came awe at the work involved, the time and energy expended by the creator. Finally, a mixture of envy and regret as the mind cast back to shriveled sunflowers and dessicated daisies, plastic flamingos and plaster Blessed Virgins. You knew well that last picture because that's what your front lawn would look like had you been less in love.

After a suitable period of grace, you would emerge from the kitchen door and stand at your accustomed place under the wood-burned sign reading not "Little Versailles", as you had suggested, but *Versailles*. The guests would move through the final arch of palm and snapdragon onto the perfect circle of bluegrass to face you both framed by cerise clematis. This was the interview corner where your wife accepted with winning modesty her deserved veneration, and you said how proud you were of her and confessed that your pet name for her was Ruby Begonia. Garden club members, new neighbors, Kiwanians, high school botany classes, even the superannuated garden page editors for the *Times* or the *Citizen* always responded with a polite chuckle.

You loved your Ruby very much; you hoped it showed. You admired her industry and were struck nearly every day by some brilliant new truth in her realm. You appreciated her tact; she only worked while you were at the office, never in the evenings, never on weekends. Although she was obsessed with her garden, she never ran on about it, never let it come between you and her. If one had to be obsessed, you reasoned, what better Siren than Beauty?

It was your conviction that her garden eased the pain of childlessness. In the winter when homework littered other dining room tables, you and she pored over seed catalogs, planning the spring showing. She consulted you earnestly, but you both knew that she would fill out the order blanks. Yes, there were disagreements. She cried on that June afternoon when you brought home the pink swans "to set off the petunias". You returned them for full credit the following day. And there was the summer she had the guest brochures printed. She gave them out just once, to the Jay Cees, then felt the distance when you stood together in front of the clematis. One Saturday a month later, you came down late to find she had already gone to the Municipal Auditorium to arrange her entries for the garden show. Next to your breakfast plate were the rest of the brochures tied with a black bow. A note lay beside the sugar bowl:

Dearest,

We are very different and I sometimes wonder why God brought us together. I know why I love you. It's because of your good sense, the common kind of sense you showed the day the Jay Cees came. I didn't want the folder to be a show-off kind of thing, but that's what it turned out to be and you knew it and I felt your disapproval. Thank you for disapproving, for setting me straight even without saying anything. I know I go overboard, but sometimes I get so lonesome. The beauty of *our* garden can never be as beautiful as what was denied to us, but it is beautiful, it is my love for you in those flowers. Please forget the folder. I want you to see me as beautiful and not a bragging person. I know why I love you, but on days like this I can't figure out what you see in me.

I saw a lovely pair of marble urns at the Emporium yesterday. They would be so nice on either side of the front hall. Let me buy them so that you can put whatever you want in them. May I suggest some ruby begonias?

Another sentence had been started, then crossed out. She was obviously in a hurry to get a glimpse of the competition. It was one of the many years in which she would win a Best.

Marriage is a balancing act. Each partner responds to the other's needs in order to keep their common life in equilibrium. In the best marriages, husband and wife do not wait to react to an unsettling movement; they anticipate the imbalance and alter their stances to provide the necessary counterweight—the word of understanding, the anger at the outsider's insult, the warm caress upon the cold heart. In the practice of marriage, man and woman learn the rhythm of stability in a reeling world. They come to see the folly of rash actions that in the days of youth caused their union to totter and sometimes to fall to pieces. Putting those pieces back in place was painful, yet enlightening; they would move more deliberately next time lest give and take turn again to push and shove. Later, with God's grace there comes a day when act becomes art and balance becomes second nature, when practice makes so nearly perfect that the fear of falling is but a memory to wonder at and share a smile over.

Compassion, kindness, humility, patience, forgiveness, love—the virtues that Saint Paul praises as necessary to authentic Christian living are also those that bring balance to Christian marriage. There is another virtue not directly mentioned in the Letter to the Colossians, but strongly implied when such phrases as "let the word of Christ dwell in you", "be thankful", and "singing psalms, hymns, and spiritual songs with gratitude in your hearts" are coupled with the admonition to "persevere in prayer" (4:2). This is the symmetry of *shared* prayer. Large numbers of prayerful persons have been won over to this form of praise through the blessings God bestows upon members of Bible study and renewal groups, but how many wives and husbands have applied it to their life together?

Most couples don't consciously avoid praying together; rather, they have never realized that it is an option. Their upbringing in the Church taught them that prayer is a private manifestation of an individual relationship between creature and Creator; additional voices just confuse the dialogue between me and God. Others, who may have found consolation in praying with friends in Christ-centered groups, would blush at the idea of praying with those who should be their best friends. "Oh, my husband would never reveal his emotions like that." "My wife would constantly worry about whether she's doing it 'right'." Then there are those to whom spontaneity is an insurmountable challenge. They wouldn't know what to say or would be embarrassed at what deep, dark secrets might roll off their tongues. As a result, out of millions of partners for life who share the deepest intimacies by right and desire, only a few choose to share a simple word of praise for the One who gave them that right and desire. They are missing out on a daily miracle; some, it is reasonable to say, are missing out on a heaven-sent healing.

How many marriages swinging out of control because of lack of communication could be restored to equilibrium by ten minutes of shared prayer a day? Rather than waiting too long to react to an unsettling trend toward pride or selfishness, a husband and wife, by listening intently to each other's petitions, can mark the imbalance and reshape their approaches to a vexing question. Of course, care must be taken to avoid prayer as accusation; honest prayer seeks God's healing, not a spouse's shame. Nevertheless, a wife and husband praying together over their marital problems must be heard by the God who has espoused himself to his people. Shared prayer is not a panacea for the injuries two people can inflict upon each other, but no one can name a more powerful force for reconciliation.

For those blessed with a happy marriage, shared prayer seems a natural progression in the process that began on the day they stood before the altar. "I promise to be true to you", said each to each. Truth in Christian life is expressed must sublimely in prayer. Through the years of a marriage, truth finds its voice in many ways—words of gentleness and passion, forgiveness and fidelity. The highest truth is that wife and husband have become one according to God's plan. To offer that truth to God in each other's presence is a daily renewal of the marriage vow, the promise that God saw fit to bless. He will continue to consecrate and strengthen it each time the promise is whispered in prayer together.

❖

random fragments of matter
   collide on a sidewalk
   icy with the city's disregard
      a bruise on the ankle the size of a dime
      a ringless finger jammed
         righteous anger giving way
            to a smile

a smile and matter turns to spirit
   accident yields to hope
   sudden shyness juggles a question
      drops it offers it regrets it
      until the second stammered yes
         embraced as blushing warrant
            of intent

intent and whose was it, Lord,
   to spin these lonely hearts
   in orbits touching but once
      once on a day of every other purpose
      but jostling a stranger
         to shake out the first promise
            of love

of love and memories of blessings stretched
from timid smile across the years
to this moment made of tender yesterdays
to this shared gratitude, Lord,
this prayer echoing a life of easy friendship
we whisper and give thanks for all of it
and for a bump
Amen.

The Hypochondriac

Strengthen the hands that are feeble,
    make firm the knees that are weak,
Say to those whose hearts are frightened:
    Be strong, fear not!
Here is your God,
    he comes with vindication;
With divine recompense
    he comes to save you.
Then will the eyes of the blind be opened,
    the ears of the deaf be cleared;
Then will the lame leap like a stag,
    then the tongue of the dumb will sing.

(Isaiah 35:3–6)

There were times when Clellan Denker forgot the names of his doctors. He would wake up with a throbbing elbow, the pulse of pain weaving in his mind a wavy scene of a familiar examination room, a balding man purifying a thermometer and scribbling on a pad, and he would be drawn to that place, that man, that elusive remedy. On occasion, he would reject the picture and shuffle through others, discarding, rearranging, playing high-stakes poker with ache and relief until he found the winning combination of medicine and manner.

At work, tightness in the chest, usually striking around 11:00 a.m., could conjure a chrome and leather suite on Grand Boulevard and a battery of tests under the highly specialized eye of a figure in gray pin-stripe, or a little home in an old neighborhood for some grandfatherly advice about cutting down a bit, or a busy clinic near subsidized apartments for a brief description of his ills and a quick prescription for some pills. The final choice depended on the pace of business at the bank and on how well he wanted to feel that day. Paydays, Mondays, the quarterly audit meant a tight schedule; he couldn't be away consulting, giving blood, waiting for X-rays. Then he would choose that harried G.P. two blocks away. Most other times, though, Doreen and Patty could handle the lunch-hour traffic. He would leave the chief teller's cubicle, signal the manager, and slip out the back for a trip across the city. Loomis understood; they both could remember when the branch was a trailer.

In the beginning, Loomis would ask what was wrong, but the twenty-minute explanations became more than he could afford. It was better just to let him go, better, that is, than to watch him turn pale and gasp for air, better to welcome him back with a wave three hours later, better to see him step into the restroom clutching a small vial and emerge with a bit of color in his cheeks. For his part, Clellan Denker took for granted these easy furloughs; having worked nowhere else, he assumed such frequent absences were common given the pressures on the managerial level. Nor did he think unusual a personal consultancy of over two dozen medical men. His dear mother had convinced him as a child of his delicate constitution, and with her help, he grew accustomed to the language of diagnosis and prescription, the wisdom of second and third opinions. After her death, he continued his battle against a world of rashes, spasms, and mysterious lumps. The heavy responsibility of dealing with thousands of dollars every day only weakened his health, but he stayed on, bravely honoring the memory of his mother who, as a stockholder, had been instrumental in getting him the job. He often told Doreen and Patty of their good fortune in not being burdened with the stress of a salaried position.

Fate proved him prophetic. When the branch closed because of "changing demographics", the girls were transferred to Midtown. Loomis was downgraded to chief teller at Fairvale. Clellan Denker was terminated. The ease and frequency with which he had been able to hang up his eyeshade should have alerted him, but he always assumed that the brass wanted to maintain a presence here until the area came back to life. What would have been a shock to the most robust of men became a mortal struggle. He tore up the thirty-day notice and tried to resume his routine, but deadlines from the main office, requests for records, and the transfer of accounts sapped his will. Worst of all, since the concluding audit required his uninterrupted attendance, he could see his doctors only on weekends when they were busy, as one impatient receptionist told him, "with working people". His symptoms multiplied geometrically, feeding on each other until on the Monday after the final closing, he collapsed on his way to see an inner-ear man.

In the crowded corridor of the public hospital, he lay on a wheeled stretcher while a nurse peppered him with questions. He told her he suffered from chronic dyspepsia, night-blindness, arthritis, heart murmur, high blood pressure, occasional asthma attacks, back trouble, migraines, kidney stones, a touch of diabetes, intermittent loss of balance, several allergies, catarrh, and insomnia. She had already checked the box marked "geriatric" when she asked his age. She made him repeat it, then employed her eraser. Could he give her the name of his family physician? The pain in his chest produced shimmering scenes of waiting

177

rooms and white-coated men brandishing stethoscopes, but no names, just familiar faces flashing by. They seemed to share some secret knowledge.

Early on Friday, Doctor Evelyn Garvey wished him good morning, nodded toward the interns at the foot of the bed, and asked how he felt. His answer was to repeat what everyone within shouting distance now knew by heart: a list of seven private hospitals, any of which would accept him as an old and valued friend. With unaccustomed vigor, he demanded once more to be moved, giving voice to his barely concealed fear of public institutions, his distaste for the snoring, snorting, sneezing wretches in the other beds, his distrust of women doctors. She told him a transfer wasn't necessary since there was nothing wrong with him. As he listened incredulously to her report, his worst suspicions of medicine for the masses were confirmed; in three days of testing they hadn't discovered a hint of what his own doctors had been telling him for years. If only he could remember the name of one of them, but now that his pain had subsided, seemingly disappeared, even their faces refused to swim into view. He should have called Loomis. He had thought about his only real friend several times while being probed and pumped and drained, thought of asking him to go to his flat to get some names and addresses from his medicine bottles, but then Loomis would have seen how many there were and would have thought he was crazy. So this woman and these kids with their notebooks were his only hope, and they wouldn't treat him, wouldn't even run the tests he described, the ones his doctors always gave him.

"There are no more tests to give", she said. "We simply found a very unhealthy mixture of medication in your system. You've been off everything since your first night here. My suggestion is to . . ."

Something more than righteous indignation filled him as his mind recoiled from what he knew her advice would be. Some hidden strength, long forgotten, coursed through his limbs as he sat up straight in bed, pulled his clothes off the hook, and turned his back on them all. Tearing at buttons and zippers, he hummed and laughed and even sang a nursery rhyme to mute her recital. Only on his way out did he stop at the communal shaving mirror to look and listen, to look at a young face with rosy cheeks, to listen to an offer to sign the release here rather than being escorted to the lobby. He grabbed the clipboard and took the pen in steady fingers. The signature was not in a teller's crabbed hand but flowed across the whole page, long and looping and strong.

The papers scattered on the floor as he plunged through the door and down the hall to the elevator. It was in use, so he went to the fire stairs and ran down six flights. Once on the sidewalk, his pace slowed; he glanced into store windows at rounded shoulders slumping, stride becoming shuffle. A gum machine revealed sallow skin, puffy eyes, a series of waiting rooms with outdated magazines. He turned to confront a street vendor's display of tiny china dolls stacked in tiers on a wobbly cart and saw his medicine chest bulging with row upon row of small bottles with neatly typed instructions. On the second shelf from the bottom at the far left was a pale blue tube with dark blue capsules for dizziness. He felt dizzy.

❖

There is a soul sickness called scrupulosity that has many of the characteristics of hypochondria. Without much basis in reality, the scrupulous Christian thinks he is about to fall into sin at the slightest hint of temptation. As the life of a hypochondriac is devoted to constant vigilance against lurking drafts and runny-nosed children, so the world of the scrupulous becomes circumscribed by the fear of doing evil, hermetically sealed against exterior stimuli that might release the contagion of sin. Ironically, imprisoned by their antiseptic bubbles, these tortured souls are forced to turn inward only to find to their horror that the source of temptation lies in the human heart. The result is a severely restricted spiritual life. The freedom to exercise a Christian ministry among friend and neighbor is limited by the dread of exposure to the virus of evil. At the same time, any hope of serenity in prayer is stymied by a supposed absence of interior goodness, the heart's congenital imperfectibility. A life for others is nearly impossible when the ample endowments of my co-worker appear to be an invitation to break my marriage vows; I will not reach out to her in friendship if I cannot be sure where my hand will stop. Nor can I turn to God in prayer, for my unworthiness, my lack of purity in motive, my inability to see myself as lovable make me shrink back before Absolute Perfection.

The mistaken assumption that temptation itself is evil is a plague upon the prayer life of the scrupulous person. Here, the uninvited daydream, be it sensual, prideful, or vengeful, is much more than a time-wasting distraction. Affronting God, the harshest of judges, a tainted reverie during meditation seems to sever all contact with the One who demands purity of intention. Peace of mind, that sweet gift of authentic prayer, is unattainable when the prayer must match the perfection of the divine object. No wonder so many of the scrupulous give up on all but formula prayer. Spontaneity in any endeavor requires trust in the self; when the self is deemed a hotbed of temptation and temptation is evil, the battle is already lost. There is no consolation to be gained in entering prayer as a contest in which failure is predetermined.

The time-honored remedy for scrupulosity is to put one's relationship with God completely in the keeping of a spiritual director, to take as Gospel truth another's affirming estimation of the soul's worth and to follow without question the path indicated by an absolving hand. Unfortunately, few of us enjoy the luxury of a personal guide in matters of the spirit; we must be our own directors. The scrupulous among us thus continue to drink from poisoned wells.

Without wise spiritual counsel, there may be no permanent cure for scrupulosity, but there is a self-imposed regimen that can, with practice, lead to a markedly healthier relationship with God. This strategy makes use of the one virtue to which even the most scrupulous Christian must admit: faith. Although loath to assume credit for any moral strength, he endures the struggle because of a firm belief in the power of God. While it is true that one so afflicted dwells irrationally on divine vengeance, on a heavenly penchant for punishment, the very fear of offending God manifests a desire to please him or at least to avoid his anger. No matter how terrible God may seem, some sort of communion with him is still worth striving for. The first step in the prescription, then, is to meditate on God's raw power no matter how frightening that may be.

In praying the power of God, the scrupulous person, over a period of time and with many frights and withdrawals, comes to recognize that divine might sweeps out in all directions, taking many forms. Punishment is just one of the forms; forgiveness, healing, and acceptance are others. Daily, disciplined reading of the Gospels gives proportion to the exercise. Against the infrequent portraits of the threatening or judgmental Jesus, there stand literally hundreds of snapshots of the incarnation of God's compassion, pardon, and affirmation in his Son. The scrupulous person has concentrated too long on one valid and necessary aspect of God's power. In contextual prayer over the whole spectrum of Gospel stories, he contemplates other facets. A deliberately continuous reading of the Evangelists is best in this case, for the scrupulous have an itch to linger over the separation of the sheep and the goats. Once the sufferer is convinced that among the many powers of the Almighty is that of compassionate understanding, the second, and by far more difficult, step can be taken: acceptance of the fact that God not only has this power, but that he wants to use it.

No, we cannot pray ourselves out of scrupulosity. Neither will a lifetime of meditation on Scripture without professional guidance heal whatever forgotten traumas gave rise to the malady. But a balanced appreciation of God's power, as operative in the Son he sent to reveal himself to us, can strengthen our weak conviction concerning his *will* to save. As we observe Jesus constantly pardoning, even extending his Father's compassion to his executioners, there will come the assurance that it is God's desire to affirm and magnify what he has created. Praying God's power means growing in the confidence that "this is the will of the one who sent me, *that I should not lose anything of what he gave me*, but that I should raise it [on] the last day. For this is the will of my Father, that everyone who sees the Son and believes in him may have eternal life, and I shall raise him [on] the last day" (John 6:39–40).

❖

Sharp lightning from the mountain,
a darkling soul revealed:
too late to reconvene the night,
too late the murky shield
which offered tortured freedom
to appetites unclean,
too late to flee the searing wrath
now, God, that you have seen.

Yet he who shared your vision
infrequently did stare,
preferring to avert his eyes
from folly's baleful glare;
he peered around the evil
to goodness at the core
and with a tender look of love
sought only to restore.

O Mighty One, I beg you,
hide not the holy face
which wept upon Jerusalem
and then to guilt brought grace.
The flashing bolt of judgment
exposes pride and guile,
but swift I see in Jesus' gaze
forgiveness in a smile.
         Amen.

Us

By the streams of Babylon
    we sat and wept
    when we remembered Zion.
On the aspens of that land
    we hung up our harps,
Though there our captors asked of us
    the lyrics of our songs,
And our despoilers urged us to be joyous:
    "Sing for us the songs of Zion!"
How could we sing a song of the Lord
    in a foreign land?

                    (Psalm 137:1–4)

You weren't much for class reunions. Uneasy from the start, you wished you were shorter or that name tags were made for foreheads rather than for chests. At a business seminar or training workshop where one wasn't supposed to know anyone else, bending down to peer at a scribbled autograph was expected; the introductory mix always looked like a convention of Tyrolean apple bobbers. Reunions, however, push peripheral vision to the limit, especially for long-time exiles with cloudy memories. Who is this gaunt redhead who knows you so well, asking after your family and your airline schedule? Courtesy, not to mention panache, demanded direct eye contact and hearty generalizations. If he would just look away or sneeze or throw his head back and laugh, then you could look quickly down and back in time to say, "That's right, Bob, that's certainly true". But no, he had you locked in his sights.

184

Only when he tired of your vagueness and moved off to a more stimulating venue did you risk a glance. HI! I'M: Steve Billings. Wasn't Steve Billings a fat kid, lead trumpet in the marching band, math whiz? Or was that Sean Bingham? You looked up guiltily to be reminded from six feet away of some deviltry at a prom: a tanned, outdoorsy type with a screechy voice and a drink in each hand. Her name tag was upside down.

You knew it would be like this, knew you would spend most of the evening talking with people no longer familiar about things you couldn't remember. After the only other reunion you attended ten years ago, you vowed never again to subject yourself to those who had stuck here and saw each other daily. They had been staging a gathering like this every five years, but to them it was just another party at the country club. They weren't being tested, didn't pore over a graduation picture on a plane, didn't have to call a cab to get here. Once is enough, you had decided. Now you were here again.

Right up to the first slap on the back, you weren't sure why you had returned. Something last January made you go back to the wastebasket and retrieve the jokey announcement, something in the roar of traffic, something in the scream of sirens and clack of office machines. Although the city had treated you pretty well for twenty years, a feeling of emptiness had begun to grow as the kids went off to college. Their escape reminded you of your own flight from conventionality, of that blessed rootlessness that comes with being away from home. You saw in their eyes the gleam of experiment, of unhobbled choice, then looked hard in the mirror and came sadly to reaffirm what the years had taught, that the pristine promise of freedom so prized by youth soon becomes adulterated. Maybe that's what *adult* meant: tarnished. This amorphous cloud of hopes permanently disfigured magnified a certain coldness, a sharpened aloofness in the rumble of the city last winter that made you finally sign the reply form, compose a properly humble status report for the souvenir booklet, and call the airline. The message wasn't crystal clear, but it was chilly enough to provoke dreams of home fires burning.

"Hello. I'm Rick Phillips. Where are you now?"

Thank God. That's the way it should be done. Could he have had a workshop in reunions? You spoke about the stock market, the presidential campaign, and the weather. He was in sales, an electronics company in Cleveland. Who was he? Basketball player? It must have been the team that went to State. Suddenly that train ride home after the final loss blotted out professional geniality. His paean to microchips gave way to your breathless description of the tears and the anger and the whole car full of kids emptying onto the platform singing the fight song . . . and Rick, weeping uncontrollably, cradling the consolation trophy.

"Wasn't that a night, Rick? Just as if we had won."

"Uh, well, I'm Peggy's husband. Peggy Smallwood? I didn't go to Central."

He didn't go to Central. He wasn't one of . . . of us. Is that what the city had been saying about you? Not one of us. After twenty years, after three kids and a backbreaking mortgage and the slippery corporate ladder and countless congenitally indecisive community boards, you still weren't one of us because in the city nobody is one of us. Jackhammers and conference calls and typewriters all singing the same song: among these six million, you are absolutely free to be whoever you want to be, but not one of us, because in the city there is no us.

It was time for the program. Yearbook predictions, innocent parodies, a short talk by the honored teacher, prizes

186

for most children and least hair, all in the flat twang you tried for so long to disguise. As usual, it was a hometown production, too difficult to arrange these things by letter. One by one they stood and made their neighbors laugh. Beneath their words you heard the assurance; they knew who they were and where they were. The boys and girls you grew up with had become the town, were now responsible for keeping the peace, selling the cars, building the houses. Ten years ago they were just taller children; by tonight they had become us. It was our park and our Chestnut Street and our life. Mrs. Franklin, seventy-two and still teaching world history, finished her last anecdote and introduced the Alma Mater. Chairs scraped. Your eyes filled up.

In the motel room, you decided not to call Connie. Her city voice would drive away the suddenly sweet accents that had bid you good night and Godspeed. Instead, you lay on the bed, idly scanning the thin telephone book. There were the name tags you had been too self-conscious to look at, names of rooted men and women who made the town work, accountable people rightfully residing at addresses set solidly in the good, hard granite of a piece of the earth nobody you knew had ever heard of. You spoke the names aloud, conjuring pimply faces and crewcuts, houses with porches and rock-walled basements. They were all still here, in this their place, and would be tomorrow as you sat with the drone of a jet engine in your ear, waiting to unfasten your seat belt and plunge again into a world that was never your own.

The paperweight gleamed on the night table. Plastic alabaster with a small brass plate: *Longest Distance*. You could still hear the applause as you stood up, still see the faces of the exiles bending toward each other whispering "Who's that?". The regulars didn't have to ask. They knew all those

187

who were not of them. Longest Distance. They would never know how long.

❖

That which is most poignant in special gatherings of old friends or family members usually occurs beneath the surface, suppressed by tacit agreement. We take our harps from the aspens, strike warmly reminiscent chords, sing of auld lang syne, but mute our thoughts of the future for fear of spoiling the harmony. There is a rhythm to reunions—reacquaintance, remembrance, contentment—a measured stress that defines the best as having passed. Left unsung are our musings upon a final homecoming. I may envision the day when your place in the circle will be empty, but I would not dilute the spirit of fellowship by raising the specter of mortality.

Speculation is not on the program. What is to come lacks definition while reunions are about facts, highly colored, to be sure, but concrete and quantifiable: it all started when Mother backed the car over the hydrant; the storm hit on the night of October 3rd; we camped out in Whitewater Park. Yet all are aware that apart from the rosy security of good cheer and tendentious comparisons with the present, there runs a river leading to an uncertain horizon. Most reunions hug the shore, anchored in calm coves away from the turbulent current of time hidden beneath the ripples of the everyday. There is one such gathering, however, that deliberately celebrates the meaning of the always moving depths. It is the worshiping assembly circling the table of the Lord.

The eucharistic banquet is nothing if not a reunion. Here the faithful meet to recall the old stories of valor and cowardice, heartbreak and hope. The book of memories is opened, comparisons are made, example is enshrined. Then, gradually, this gathering parts company with more secular assemblies, for in the midst stand unseen the story-tellers of a hundred exiles, reminding us that there was never an age when we were not expatriates, storm-tossed sailors cast adrift from our moorings to make a journey on the inexorable tide.

This reunion is different. Despite the attraction of the golden days of saints and heroes, we are not borne backward; rather, there is a force present that propels us forward. That force is the power and person of the living Christ, the Omega-man, wrapped in time, who recapitulates all that has gone before, the God-man, mantled in eternity, through whom all is made new. In him, our fear of what might be is transformed into a confident vision of the final homecoming. More than a commemoration of the past, the Eucharist is an articulation of what must remain unspoken in more mundane meetings. It is nothing less than a "Yes", a communal affirmation in word and song and action of things to come, things unknown and unknowable, things accessible only to faith. At this table stands the guarantor of our hopes, offering you and me a taste of what can be ours if we will embrace his future.

In essence, all prayers are prayers of exile inasmuch as they lead to the offering of the worshiping assembly; there, no matter how private or expedient, they are gathered into the declaration of the divine host: "This is my body", to be given up that I and mine may more readily return home. "This is my blood", to be poured out as a sign of detachment from anything that might hinder the final journey.

As the dispossessed in Babylon came together to plead for freedom and dream of a renewed Jerusalem, so we assemble to shape a common petition for release from our bondage. Unlike them, however, we do not refuse the invitation to take up our harps and raise our voices in song, for we have seen the promise fulfilled. Our Jerusalem is not empty streets and echoing palaces but a vibrant city peopled by faithful forebears, governed by the firstborn from the dead who has gone ahead to prepare a place for us, a place at his table. We rejoice because this table is already ours, rough-hewn from the earth yet bearing the bread of heaven, the food of all who will admit their exile. Those rooted in this world will seek no nourishment here, for they drink too deeply of today. We are inspired by yesterday and feed on tomorrow. Even while doubting, even while fascinated by the self-assurance of those who make their home and their heaven on this seemingly solid earth, we feed on tomorrow, on the promise of the host, for we have seen Jesus' victory and yearn to share in his return.

Apart from the hopeful assembly, from the table set in heaven, we find our favorite haven for solitary meditation and consciously offer the prayer of exile. It springs from the Spirit's gift of wisdom, that divinely inspired recognition that we are strangers in a strange land, that urgent insight that directs our thoughts to the final reunion and to the rehearsal for that homecoming that is offered each Sunday in our neighborhood church. We plead for unity here and hereafter, that friend and foe alike might be blessed with the realization that home is where the heart is and that our hearts are restless until they rest in the One who has gone ahead yet still remains to guide his pilgrim people. Our purpose is to free our earthbound brothers and sisters from a prison city destined to fall to dust. Our prayer is the joyous cry of the wanderer who sees a light on the horizon. Our reward is the ingathering of exiles standing before the golden doors swung wide.

❖

sotto voce
shaded faces
just beyond an earthling's narrow view
   whisper in familiar tones
      waiting
      anticipating
      swelling with the secret
comrades risen from their bones
   match my timid step
      along the shadowed avenue

now I hear it
friends dispatched
to lead a pilgrim's hesitant return
   sing of the revealing light
      gleaming
      disclosing beaming
      smiles among my escorts
certain in the waning night
   joyful with the anthem
      which will soon be mine to learn

heed my prayer Lord
sung in concord
with the grateful hymn of those who guide
   exiles to the throne of grace
      raising
      strong voices praising
      heaven's invitation
with this psalm I take my place
   next to rescued sons and daughters
      gathered at your side
         Amen.

A Final Moment

The timelessness of prayer is entered into more readily by those who understand that time can be both a tyrant and a benefactor. That aspect of time known as the present manifests itself in the schedules and deadlines that chain us to the everyday; it tolerates no flight to freedom, dismisses as impractical anything that does not further what the world calls industry or progress. The praying person must struggle against this demanding overseer to gain control of precious moments within which the soul might take wing.

Those motivated by will power and need, who are successful in wresting a few minutes from the tyrant, find that time can reveal a friendlier face. The remembrance of things past, whether a day or a decade ago, allows the persistent Christian a clearer view of God's involvement in human affairs and brings to life the welcome assurance that he is present amid the insistent dictates of the imperious now. Thus, time can be used against itself in a dialectic leading eventually to the timelessness of union with God. As in the working out of personal salvation, so in that brief foreshadowing of salvation called personal prayer: we come to the Creator by making use of all his creation—including time—to escape time.

Praying in time, then, is making a place in the present that will allow the supplicant to cast back in his history to a moment of high drama or low humor where God seemed to be absent or at least aloof, to season that moment with the salt of subsequent experience in order to taste the compassion, the forgiveness, the protection, and the affirmation that flows from the loving presence of our Guide and our Goal. In these pages, we have forsaken the tyranny of minute-by-minute detail to fathom the providence that enfolded us as we moved with mixed emotions to a new house or toiled to bring in the harvest or hesitantly gathered with half-forgotten friends. Each meditation has provided a revelation of God's mercy, prompting us to speak to him in wonder and gratitude for what he has done and what he is doing. Because we have seen him in our times, we know he is with us in this time.

Our today is made holy by our yesterdays. Our now, this moment between tick and tock, becomes what the ancient Greeks called *kairos*, an especially favorable time for an undertaking, in this case, the sublime undertaking known as prayer. If the aim of this book has been fulfilled, if we have indeed achieved authentic prayer through the recollection of blessed memories, then we have known the timelessness of communion with God and will know it again.

There is more, however, something that the astute reader recognized early on: the title of this book has another meaning. Besides struggling against the clamor of the world to pray in this day and this time, besides using those times of our lives called personal history to appreciate and confirm God's loving presence, each of us must pray in time, that is, before the chance is lost. This mandate has nothing to do with begging for heaven's rescue before the last trumpet sounds; rather, it is based upon a conclusion arising from even the most cursory examination of the vignettes herein, namely, that many of the players in these scenes, apparently good folks concerned for their own welfare and the common weal, that these people burdened by anxiety and buoyed by joy, did not pray. They did not step away from detail, deadline, or danger to seek the timeless presence of God in their own time.

"Persevere in prayer", says Saint Paul to the Romans (12:12) and to the Colossians (4:2). To the Thessalonians, "Pray without ceasing" (1 Thessalonians 5:17) and to Timothy, "In every place the men should pray" (1 Timothy 2:8). In this, he was only following the heartfelt plea of his Master: "Then [Jesus] told them a parable about the necessity for them to pray always" (Luke 18:1). In too many instances, the people in these stories forgot the biblical imperative. At a moment of heightened consciousness when they were stimulated by fear, enervated by routine, or elevated by joy, they turned inward to seek communion with and surcease through the self rooted in time instead of turning outward to seek communion with the One who stands astride time. These people lost a great chance, a chance to mount to God when they were most vulnerable to his grace. These people were you and I, for these are our memories.

Christ urges constancy in prayer, and the Apostle echoes that injunction, to save us from forfeiting the opportunity to make a bit of the now timeless. To pray in time is to transform crisis into possibility, to make of mere circumstance a vehicle for deepening our union with the divine. Here is the final lesson of this book: after recognizing the unending claims of time and struggling to find a prayer place among them, after making use of memory and seasoned wisdom to recall and confirm God's presence in your personal history, apply this experience to today's trials and triumphs. Pray to a timeless God who is here, now, as he was there, then.

"Behold, now is a very acceptable time;
behold, now is the day of salvation."

(2 Corinthians 6:2)